I0609309

Clement Moore Butler

The Reformation in Sweden

Its rise, progress, and crisis; and its triumph under Charles IX

Clement Moore Butler

The Reformation in Sweden
Its rise, progress, and crisis; and its triumph under Charles IX

ISBN/EAN: 9783337383909

Printed in Europe, USA, Canada, Australia, Japan

Cover: Foto ©ninafisch / pixelio.de

More available books at **www.hansebooks.com**

The Reformation in Sweden

*ITS RISE, PROGRESS, AND CRISIS;
AND ITS TRIUMPH UNDER
CHARLES IX.*

BY

C. M. BUTLER, D.D.

*Professor of Ecclesiastical History in the Divinity School of the
Protestant Episcopal Church, Philadelphia*

NEW YORK
ANSON D. F. RANDOLPH & COMPANY
900 BROADWAY, COR. 20th STREET

CONTENTS.

CONTENTS.

CHAPTER VII.

CHAPTER VIII.

CHAPTER IX.

CHAPTER X.

CHAPTER XI.

CHAPTER XII.

THE REFORMATION IN SWEDEN.

CHAPTER I.

SWEDEN FROM THE TREATY OF CALMAR, 1398, TO THE INVASION OF CHRISTIAN II. OF DENMARK, 1520.

THE history of Scandinavia, previous to the union of the three kingdoms of Denmark, Sweden and Norway, under Queen Margaret, in accordance with the treaty of Calmar, is a record of violent commotions and revolutions, and of incessant wars between the three kingdoms. There is very little in it to repay the student of general history for the time and toil it will cost him to acquire any coherent idea of its ever-shifting conditions, and still less to attract or reward the student of ecclesiastical history.

Scandina-via previous to Treaty of Calmar, 1398. The reigns of Birger, 1290–1319, and of his son Magnus, 1319–1363, in Sweden, were so marked by cruelty and disaster to the nation that some of the banished nobles invited Albert, Count of Mecklenburg, son of the sister of Magnus, to invade the kingdom and take possession of the throne. He accepted the invitation and succeeded to the throne and reigned from 1363 to 1389. But his favors to Germans so offended the native nobility that they compelled him to dismiss his German favorites, and to accept one of their number, Bo Jonsson, as his chief adviser in the government.

Jonsson soon became his master, and his heirs offered the throne to Margaret, Queen of Denmark and Norway. She sent an army into Sweden, which defeated and captured and imprisoned Albert. As Albert's son died in 1379 there was no one to contest Queen Margaret's claim to the throne, and the designation of her nephew Eric, Duke of Pomerania, to succeed to the triple throne of Denmark, Norway and Sweden, which was secured by the treaty of Calmar, in 1398.

Sweden un-der Queen Margaret. The conditions upon which the union of the three kingdoms was concluded were such as seemed to promise peace and many mutual advantages. It promised to put an end to the feuds by which the Scandinavian kingdoms had hitherto been convulsed, and to give to each member of the confederacy, while still retaining its separate laws and customs, a strength beyond its own to resist the encroachments of more powerful states. It provided that the election of the king should in future be made conjointly, —the sons of the sovereign being preferred; each realm was to be governed by its own laws; fugitives from one country were not to be protected in another; all were bound to take up arms for the common defence.

It is obvious to remark how great would have been the advantages of such an arrangement if it could have been faithfully maintained; but it is equally obvious to conclude that such a union of rival states is scarcely practicable in the most advanced stages of civilization, and quite impossible at an era of violence and under an undefined system of succession to the throne. Margaret herself introduced, or rather set in motion, the existing elements of discord by her partiality to her Danish subjects,—to whom she committed the chief posts and fortresses of Sweden,—by her new and heavy

imposts, her prodigality to the clergy, and her avowed
policy of humbling the nobles of the land. The inevitable result immediately ensued—hatred on the
part of the Swedes and devotion on the part of the
Danes. By a native historian of Sweden she is said to
have been regarded by the Danes as *sanctam et canoni-
zatione dignam*, and by the Swedes as *profundissimo
dignam inferno*.

*Sweden un-
der King
Eric.*
The discontent of the Swedes broke out
into open rebellion after the death of Queen
Margaret and the accession of King Eric.
The king was not qualified either by his character or
his administrative ability to conciliate the esteem, or
to silence the dissatisfaction of his subjects. His cruel
treatment of his wife Phillippa of England, who by
her gentleness and intelligence won the hearts of the
Swedes, subjected him to deserved obloquy. In the
pursuit of objects in which Sweden had no interest—
the recovery of his dukedom of Pomerania and the
fruitless attempt to conquer Schleswig—he exhausted
the resources of the country and shed the blood of his
subjects in wars from which they could reap no benefit. This continued drain of men and money from the
kingdom, and the oppression of the Danes and Germans, who filled all the offices and occupied all the
castles of the land, led to a civil war, which, checked
from time to time, still broke out afresh, and was to be
extinguished only after a hundred years of discord and
bloodshed by the disruption of the union between Denmark and Sweden.

*Rising of
Englebert in
Dalecarlia.*
Englebert Englebertson, an intelligent, eloquent and popular miner of Dalecarlia, who
had passed his youth in the household of
great barons, and had there acquired a degree of

knowledge and culture superior to that which was usual in his class, vowed to avenge the injuries suffered by the Dalecarlians in common with all their countrymen. The government of that province was in the hands of a Danish nobleman named Ericson. His administration was marked by every species of brutal cruelty and oppression. Englebert proceeded to Denmark and laid before the king proofs of the atrocious tyranny of Ericson. The king ordered an inquiry to be made, and the charges were admitted by the State Council to have been sustained. Armed with their report, Englebert returned to Denmark and laid it before the king and demanded the removal and punishment of Ericson. But the king had changed his mind, and ordered Englebert to be gone and never again to appear in his presence. Eric replied—" Yet once more I will return."

The report of this reception by the king was the signal for revolt. The Dalesmen rose, elected Englebert to be their leader, marched against Westeras in the autumn of 1433, and though induced to retire by some of the State Council who were there, by their promise to urge reforms, yet they would not disperse before taking an oath that they never again would pay taxes to Ericson. An attempt on the part of Ericson to collect the taxes led to a second insurrection; but the State Council having persuaded Ericson to resign his command, the Dalesmen were again appeased. Ericson himself took refuge in the monastery of Wadstena, from which, two years after, he was dragged out by the peasantry and put to death.

This was the first armed resistance to the Danish dynasty, which continued from this period, 1433, at intervals and with varying fortunes, and with several revolutions, until at length, under Gustavus Vasa, and by his agency, Sweden became, and has since continued independent of Denmark.

Accession of Christian II. of Denmark. It was necessary to describe the circumstances under which Sweden became subject to the crown of Denmark, in order to understand the history of Gustavus Vasa, who both liberated Sweden from the sway of Denmark and introduced and established Protestantism in his kingdom. But it is not important, as preparatory to a sketch of the Reformation in Sweden, to narrate the civil history of the interval between the treaty of Calmar and the accession of Christian II. A mere outline of those events will answer for our present purpose. Suffice it to say that Englebert was elected Regent of the Kingdom, and held the position for three years; that he was succeeded in that position by another patriot, Karl Knutson, who was subsequently elected king; that the dynasty of Denmark again came into power in Sweden and held it nominally and sometimes for a brief period actually, during the reign of Christian I., 1448–81, and of Hans or John, 1481–1513, who was succeeded by Christian II. in the latter year. From this point the history of the Reformation in Sweden properly begins.

Reigns of Christian I. and John. The supremacy of the kings Christian I. and John in Sweden was rather nominal than real. The real power was exercised by patriotic Swedes for the most part, who were repeatedly at war with Denmark. Under a popular native nobleman, Sten Sturé, nephew of their former king, Karl Knutson, as regent, Sweden enjoyed for some few years comparative peace and prosperity. But in consequence of evils which fell upon the kingdom, for which he was in no degree responsible—such as a succession of bad crops, and the excommunication pronounced against him, because in the interests of the state he withheld the revenues claimed by the Danish Queen dowager—Sturé became unpopular with the fickle and unreasoning people. The king availed himself of this dissatisfaction, and the consequent depression of the kingdom, to march an army into Sweden with a view to establish his personal authority. The expedition of King John was successful; and he was crowned in Stockholm on the 25th of November, 1497. Sturé was deposed from the Regency, but became High Chancellor, and was one of the four commissioners to whom the administration of the kingdom was committed, by King John, on his return to Denmark. But on account of the great dissatisfaction with King John's administration, in 1501 Sturé was again placed at the head of the government with the name of Guardian of the Kingdom. This position he held until his death, December 15, 1503. He was succeeded in the same office by his kinsman, Saunto Sturé, whose administration of nine years was an incessant but successful series of wars, in resistance of the efforts of King John to regain supremacy in the kingdom. After his death in 1512, his son, Steno Sturé, was called by the popular voice, rather than by any recognized authority, as his successor. 'His election was subsequently forced upon the council at Stockholm by the popular clamor.

Death of King John —Accession of Christian II. Christian II., justly known as "the tyrant," succeeded King John, who died in 1513. He immediately opened negotiations with the Guardian and the Council with a view to secure their recognition of his right to the throne of Sweden. Failing in this attempt, he excited his partisan,

Trollé, the Archbishop, to organize an armed rebellion in his interest against the existing government. The Archbishop was described as one "who never forgave a past wrong, real or fancied." It in no degree disarmed his hostility that Sture, in order to bring about a reconciliation, had secured his election to the Archbishopric. He stirred up war therefore in the interest of Christian II., who upon the invasion of Sweden, suffered a complete defeat. This battle, as celebrated in Swedish annals as that of Bannockburn in the history of Scotland, was fought at Bren-Kirka, July 22, 1518. It was in this battle that Gustavus Vasa first appeared prominently, having occupied the honorable position of standard bearer, and distinguished himself for valor and ability in the field. As the history of the rise of the Reformation in Sweden turns upon that of Gustavus Vasa, and his history is inseparably implicated with that of Christian II., it becomes necessary to give a sketch of the life and character of each.

Christian II. Christian II. was the only son of King John and his Queen, Christina of Saxony, and was born in 1481. It is an evidence of the simplicity of the times, and of the country, that in order to provide for their frequent absence from Copenhagen, the King and Queen, instead of leaving him in the palace in the care of their own attendants, placed him under the charge of a book-binder of the City. It may be inferred also that, discerning his imperious, cruel and crafty nature, his parents felt that these evil traits would be more likely to be restrained in a well regulated private home, than in the palace, where his faults would be likely to be flattered and inflamed, rather than restrained, by subservient menials and courtiers. Hans Metzenheim, the book-binder, was a burgomaster and a counsellor of state, and having no children of their own, he and his wife devoted themselves assiduously to the education of the royal boy. His capacity was very great, and he applied himself well, under constraint, to his studies, and made rapid progress; but his tutor Hinze, a Canon of the Cathedral, dared not trust the wayward boy out of sight, and therefore, always took him to church when on duty there. As the young Prince had a fine voice and a good ear for music, he was made to sing among the choristers at matins and vespers. But when King John was told that the heir of three Kingdoms was singing, and was much admired, in all of the choirs of Copenhagen, he sharply rebuked his tutor for placing his son in a position derogatory to his royal dignity. The incident led to a change of tutors. At the request of the King, Joachin of Brandenburg sent him another tutor, Magister Conrad, a man of great learning and force of character, who was able to control his pupil, and succeeded in imbuing him with a love of learning. Christian made great progress and is said at an early age and during all his life "to have written and spoken Latin as well as the most learned University professors of his time" (Otto's Scandinavia, page 214).

But this ready mastery of learning seems in no degree to have softened or refined his character. He was accustomed, after he was domiciled in the palace, to bribe the porter to allow him to go out in the night and join in scenes of revelry and licentiousness. On some occasions, when detected in these *escapades*, the King personally applied a horse-whip to his shoulders. But when he had reached the age of twenty, and this sort of rigid discipline became no longer possible, the King sent him as his Viceroy to govern Norway. He

at once put himself in an attitude of hostility to the
nobility, and relentlessly crushed out every attempt
at resistance or rebellion. He seems from his early
boyhood to have hated the nobility, to have had a
dislike to their character, habits and manners, quite
irrespective of their feelings or relations towards himself. His chosen associates were among the lower
classes. His enmity to the nobles was increased by
the restrictions which they imposed upon his authority
at his Coronation.

Gustavus Vasa. Gustavus Vasa, or as he was called before
he became king, Gustavus Erickson, was descended from an ancient and noble family. His grandfather, Christopher Nilson, was appointed a councillor
by King Eric. His father was not distinguished in
the public service, and though called "a merry and
facetious lord," was arraigned before the council in
Stockholm for cruelty to his peasants, and made to
pledge himself "that he would not thereafter place
them in irons or treat them like senseless beasts,"
when accused of depredations upon his estates, but
"would allow them their rights in law." The date
of his birth has been fixed on good grounds, on As-
cension Day, 1496. Those presages of future greatness which seldom fail to be subsequently recorded,
in the case of those who become renowned, were not
wanting at his birth. A crimson cross was marked
upon his breast, and the outline of a helmet was seen
upon his head. When he was only four years old,
King John, during one of his later visits to Sweden,
saw him playing the part of the king in the midst of
a group of children and, as the story goes, patted him
upon the head, saying "that if he lived he would be
a remarkable man." He kept the bright boy in his

train while he was in Sweden, and wished to carry
him to Denmark. If he had done so the whole history of Northern Europe would have been changed,
the Reformation in Sweden perhaps never effected,
nor the liberation of Protestantism, mainly due to
the heroic Gustavus Adolphus, achieved. But Sten
Sturé, suspecting that the king was more bent on securing a hostage than a foster son, sent him to his
father, who was then Lord Feudatory of Aland.

Geijer remarks that "all accounts agree that young
Gustavus was placed in the Seminary of Upsala, in
1509." "It is known," he continues, "that he was
placed in the grammar school and was subjected to
personal chastisement while there by the Danish schoolmaster. The latter was informed that the young pupil
had upon some occasion said, 'See what I will do! I
will go to Dalecarlia, get out the Dalesmen, and knock
the Danes on the head.' Gustavus suffered his school
flogging, then drawing his little sword, he thrust it
through the curtains with a malison never to return.
A hundred years afterwards the country people could
point out the places in the neighborhood of Upsala
which he had frequented with his playmates, and tell
how he had been at a wolf chase hunting merrily." As
an indication of the bent of his mind toward religious
subjects, it is stated that while he was at Upsala, his
chief studies, outside of the curiculum of the school,
were canon law and theology. He was also a gifted
musician, and while at school made several musical
instruments, which are still preserved in the palace
of Stockholm.

All accounts agree that he was received and employed in the Court of the Regent Sten Sturé the
younger. He was then eighteen years of age, and was

placed under the tuition of Hemming Gadd, who had been mathematicus to Pope Alexander III., had written a history of Sweden which was much prized, was a sworn enemy of the Danes and an able politician. With him, no doubt, the young patriot could freely resume his boyish talk of his purpose to rouse up Dalesmen and knock Danes upon the head—a seemingly wild and empty boast which was subsequently so remarkably fulfilled. The chroniclers of the time speak of him as "a noble youth, comely, ready-witted and prompt in action." He was particularly distinguished, even at that early period, for the persuasive eloquence which was one of the most potent means by which he subsequently acquired such a commanding influence over his countrymen. Even to his extreme old age, when Gustavus met any large body of his countrymen in council, or in a crisis of affairs, they would clamor for a speech from the old man eloquent, and receive it with immense applause, and insist that there was no orator like him. We shall see how at a momentous crisis of his own fortunes and of those of the Reformation, he consolidated the former and saved the latter by a single speech.

The battle of Brenn-Kirk. It was after Gustavus had resided at the court three years, that the rising of Archbishop Trollé, in the interest of Christian II., already alluded to, occurred. The Archbishop was besieged in his castle of Stekborg and a Danish reinforcement was sent to his relief. This force was defeated by Gustavus. In the following year, in the famous battle of Brenn-Kirk, between King Christian and Sten Sturé, in which the king was defeated, Gustavus, as we have seen, bore the banner. But by the treachery of the king, and the misplaced confidence in him of the Regent, this victory resulted in disaster and loss rather than gain. The Danes attempted after the defeat to retreat, but the fleet in which they embarked their shattered forces was detained by contrary winds, and sorely pressed by famine. The king, in order to gain time, professed a desire to negotiate a peace which should leave Sweden henceforth unmolested by the Danes. The Regent, feeling that he had the king in his power, and that he could force upon him terms which would secure him and his kingdom in the future, consented to treat with him; and during the negotiations he generously furnished the famishing squadron with beef and other provisions. The king invited him to a personal conference on board his ship; and the unsuspecting Regent would have fallen into the snare thus prepared for him, had not the town council declared that if he went on board they would soon have another Regent, for they were sure he never would return.

Foiled in this base design, the king devised another, equally treacherous, which was completely successful. He professed his willingness to come on shore, provided suitable hostages should be sent to the squadron. Six nobles—including Gustavus and Hemming Gadd —were chosen for this purpose. But the boat in which they were embarked, had not accomplished half its passage to the fleet, when a Danish ship with a hundred men on board captured it, and carried the six hostages to the fleet as prisoners. A favorable breeze springing up took away all hope of rescue. The fleet weighed anchor, the sails were filled, and they were all soon landed on the coast of Denmark. Thus the defeated king, by an act of gross treachery, evaded the promised proposals of peace, provisioned his starving fleet and army from his victorious enemy, and carried into captivity six of the most eminent nobles of the land. But it was a triumph which, by intensifying the patriotic passion of the Swedes, led to an ultimate defeat.

The Captivity and escape of Gustavus. Gustavus had the good fortune to be committed to the care of a kinsman, Baron Eric Baner, Governor of the castle of Kallö, North Jutland, where he spent upwards of a year as a prisoner, and was treated with kindness and allowed a liberty, not usually granted to prisoners of state. But the whole country was ringing with rumors of the great preparations which were in progress for the conquest of Sweden. Christian had imposed new taxes for the prosecution of the war and even extorted from the Papal Legate the sums that had been amassed by the sale of indulgences, which he appropriated on the plea that it was a war in which the interests of the Papacy were involved. Copenhagen was thronged with French, Scotch and English mercenary officers and troops. The young soldiers at the mess of the castle of Kallö talked of the preparations for the conquest of Sweden with exasperating exultation. They boasted that they would soon play with the Swedes "S. Peter's game"—an allusion to the Papal interdict which they hoped to secure, and jestingly and mockingly parcelled out among themselves the wealth and beauty of the nation.

How the ardent and patriotic heart of the young Gustavus must have chafed in his captivity! "By such contumelies was Lord Gustavus Ericson seized with anguish beyond measure, so that neither meat nor drink might savor pleasantly to him, even if he had been furnished better than he was. His sleep was neither quiet nor delectable, for he could think of noth-, ing else than how he might find opportunity to extricate himself from the unjust captivity in which he was held" (Geijer, page 98).

It is not to be wondered at that under such circumstances Gustavus should have persuaded himself that he might without dishonor escape from his captivity. He might well feel that he was called to do so by duty to his country. He was not a prisoner captured in war. He was stolen and consigned to captivity in violation of Royal pledges and of the laws which regulated the warfare of civilized nations. Early in the morning of February 19, he left the castle disguised, according to some as a pilgrim, but according to others as a drover, and traveled on the first day of his escape forty-two English miles. He did not reach Lubeck until the last day of September, when he threw himself on the protection of the Burgomaster and Council. As soon as Eric Baner discovered the retreat of Gustavus, he hastened to Lubeck, armed with a letter of the King, and demanded back his prisoner. He complained at the same time that Gustavus had escaped, contrary to his pledged word as a Knight and a Kinsman. Gustavus spoke in his own defense. "I was captured," he said, "contrary to all justice and plighted faith. It is notorious that I went to the King's fleet as a hostage. Let any one who can, point out the place where I was made prisoner in battle, or declare the crime for which I deserve chains. Call me not then a prisoner, but a man seized, unjustly, overreached and betrayed. Am I not in a free city and before a government renowned for justice and for befriending the persecuted? Shall I be altogether deceived in the confidence I have reposed in them? Or can breach of faith be reasonably objected to me by one who never kept oath or promise? Or can it be wondered at that I should free myself from a prison which I deserved by no fault except that of trusting to a King?"

Gustavus promised to repay to Baner the $6,000 by which he was pledged to Christian for the security of his prisoner. This promise he was not able at first to fulfil, and subsequently he believed himself exonerated from it by the wrongs which he had endured. He denied also that he had given any pledge to remain at Kallö, or that he was in the position of a prisoner on his parole of honor.

However much or little the shrewd burgesses of Lubeck may have felt the force of this argument, their sympathies no doubt were enlisted on the side of a fine, spirited young man, the dupe of a faithless tyrant. Moreover, motives of policy happily coincided with those of feeling. Christian, as the undisputed Lord of the three Northern Kingdoms, would possess a power which he might easily employ for the subjection of one of the smallest of the free Hanse towns, which was protected rather by a tradition of its inviolability than by any possession of military power. The Burgomaster urged this view upon his colleagues. "Who knows," said the council, "What Gustavus may do when he gets back to Sweden?" They evidently hoped that he might be an instrument for checking the progress of the King in his native land, and thus prevent him from plotting against their liberties. With this view they refused to deliver Gustavus to the Baron Baner, and determined to send him back to Sweden.

His brief residence in Lubeck exercised a momentous influence on the subsequent career of Gustavus. It

was there that he first heard and became interested
in the doctrines of the Reformation, and thus became
providentially prepared for his great mission—the de-
liverance of his country from the Papal despotism.

The Inter- During the captivity of Gustavus events of
dict. the utmost moment had occurred in Sweden.
The talk of the young soldiers over their cups in the
dinner hall of Kallö, which had so exasperated him
and led to his escape, was not all boyish gasconade.
The "Game of S. Peter"—the threatened interdict—
had been played, and Sweden was soon after success-
fully invaded by Christian.

The only ground on which the Pope could claim
that there was cause for his interference between
Christian and the Swedes, was that the latter were
in rebellion against their lawful lord; and that it was
his duty to coerce kings to perform their civil duties
by spiritual penalties. There was as yet no question
of religion involved in the strife. But the once terrible
instruments of interdict and excommunication had not
lost all their power, and the former was laid upon the
kingdom, and the latter was pronounced against the
Regent, and against all who had espoused his cause.
Pope Leo X. was equally ready to pronounce a blessing or a curse which would replenish his treasury, and
enable him to indulge his luxurious tastes. No real
influence appears to have been exerted by these spiritual weapons. That in which the sting of the Papal
Bull was contained was the fact that the execution of it
was committed to Christian. It was this unusual provision which constituted the plea for the horrible atrocities which he committed when he acquired the possession of the kingdom.

CHAPTER II.

Christian's invasion of Sweden. THE whole of the year 1519 was spent in making preparations for the invasion. In the beginning of the year 1520 the Danish army broke into Sweden under the General Otho Krumpen. He caused the Papal Ban to be affixed to all the churches on his march. The Regent met the invaders on the ice of the lake of Ascunden in West Gothland. But being wounded in the beginning of the battle, he was carried out of the conflict and his army was defeated. Learning that the victorious Danes were marching upon Stockholm, he caused himself to be carried to the Capital on a sledge, but died upon the ice of lake Mälar when near the city. Everything was thrown into confusion by this disaster. A few magnates met but did not feel authorized to appoint a successor to the Regency. The country people assembled in various localities to resist the enemy; but without leaders and organization, they were easily dispersed. The heroic widow of the Regent, Christina Gillenstierna, still continued to defend Stockholm. She refused to accede to the agreement which the Swedish barons in a diet had made with Christian, that they would recognize him as king, on condition that he should govern in accordance with the laws of the kingdom and the treaty of Calmar.

Gustavus in Sweden. It was while these disasters were occurring in Sweden that Gustavus embarked in a merchant vessel bound to Stockholm, with the purpose of offering his services to the Regent's widow. Unable to penetrate into the city, because it was so closely invested, he steered for Calmar, which still held out against the king. That fortress also was defended by a woman, Ann Bielke, the widow of the former commandant. But so dispirited did he find the burghers of that city, that his appeals to them to make a gallant defense, not only failed to rouse their courage, but led to threats against his life. He fled from the city on the day that it was surrendered. From Calmar he proceeded to Småland, among his father's tenants. But even there he was not safe. The province of East Gothland was so filled with Danes, that it was only by continual changes of quarters and disguises that he escaped detection. His appeals to his countrymen to rise and shake off the yoke, were met by a stolid half-despair, which seemed now to have taken possession of all ranks in the kingdom. During the whole summer he glided through by-ways from one place of danger to another, sleeping one night in the woods, and another hidden by brush wood in the open field, disguised and pursued with a price upon his head. In September he appeared without money and with only the tattered clothes which he wore, in the house of his brother-in-law, J. Brahe. In vain he urged Brahe to disobey the summons which he had received to be present at the coronation of Christian at Stockholm, which had then surrendered. The unhappy man, sharing the terror that everywhere prevailed, feared that he would be marked if he should be absent, and set out upon the journey which proved to be, as Gustavus had predicted, his last. His son, in his chronicle of these times, gives his answer to the appeal of Gustavus: "I am specially cited to the coronation," he said, "and if I should remain away what would become of my wife and children? Perhaps ill might come of it to your parents as well as hers, and others of our friends. For you the matter stands quite otherwise, for not many know where you are. It can go no worse with me than with all the Swedish lords who are now gathered about the king." How fatally it went with both him and them we soon shall see!

Proceedings of Chris- tian. The diet of Swedish Barons held at Upsala had agreed to accept Christian as King, on the explicit condition that he would govern according to the treaty of Calmar and the laws of Sweden. These engagements were personally confirmed by the king upon arriving with his fleet before Stockholm. He added moreover that the measures adopted against Archbishop Trollé, who was now restored to his office, should be forgotten and forgiven. These assurances were again renewed when Hemming Gadd, who had spent his life in passionate opposition to the Danish claims, now appeared in old age through the depression caused by the seeming hopelessness of further resistance, as their advocate. It was by the weight of his character and the previously known hostility to the Danes, that Christina Gillenstierna was induced to surrender Stockholm, against the remonstrances of the burghers. When the king returned in autumn and was crowned in Stockholm, he once more confirmed, by oath and the reception of the Sacrament, the securities which he had given. And yet at that very moment it is placed beyond all doubt that he had resolved upon the murder of the chief nobles and highest citizens of Sweden. In the proclamation of the

council of State, issued after Christian had been dethroned, it is stated that at the coronation, and only
three days preceding the massacre of the nobles, he
had appeared, full of courtesy and friendliness, to his
unsuspecting victims. "He appeared," says that document, "friendly to all and was very merry and pleasant in his demeanor, caressing some with hypocritical
kisses, and others with embraces, clapping his hands,
and displaying on all hands tokens of affection."

It soon appeared how much had been meant by the
threat to play the game of S. Peter in Sweden, and by
leaving the execution of the Papal power in the hands
of the king. Notwithstanding the festivities and courtesies connected with the coronation, some circumstances took place which excited the suspicions of the
Swedish nobles. There was a marked omission of all
Swedes from the honors which were distributed on that
occasion. Many of the Danish officers who had sig-
nalized themselves in the invasion of the kingdom, received the honor of knighthood at the hands of the
king; but no Swede received any mark of favor beyond
empty and hypocritical courtesies and words. The
king excused himself for not extending the same hon-
or to the Swedes, on the ground that he had received
no aid from them in the recovery of the throne; but he
added that by their fidelity in the future, he would
be able to confer on them as much favor as he had
bestowed on the most distinguished of his Danish
officers.

In the midst of these festivities which lasted three
days the king held a cabinet council in which the question was discussed as to the penalties which should be
inflicted upon those who had resisted his authority by
armed rebellion. He observed that the Swedes were

exceedingly jealous of their freedom, and that unless they were completely subdued, they would not long endure a government which from its nature, in order to be effective, must be strict. He proposed to root out, as he had done in Norway, the distinguished and noble families, and leave only the commonalty, which without able leaders would soon be brought into submission. He demanded of his counsellors how this might be accomplished with the greatest safety.

Some suggested that a quarrel should be got up between the military and the town's people, and that in the confusion which would ensue, they should take off whom they pleased. But this was dismissed as a hazardous and doubtful scheme. Others suggested that gunpowder should be placed under the castle, and that a charge of treason founded upon this fact should be laid against the nobles. But the counsel of Didric Slaghec (called after this by a slight change of pronunciation *Slag-höch, or slaughter-hawk*) was that which was finally adopted. He was the king's confessor, a Westphalian by birth, and had once been a barber's assistant. He suggested—and it was believed, by a previous understanding with the king—that the king now wielded two swords, the temporal and the spiritual: the temporal in his own right and the spiritual upon the express designation of the Pope. The king might forgive offenses against himself, but not against the Holy See. His promise of oblivion was therefore to be kept as far as he personally was concerned, but in his capacity as representative of the Church it was not binding. Let him then bring the excommunication into play, and deal with all who had taken part against Archbishop Trollé as heretics. And yet the penalty which the Pope, in whose name this atrocious advice

was given, had already pronounced was only that the
demolished castle of the archbishop should be rebuilt,
and that compensation for damages should be given,
and a pecuniary fine should be levied.

"The blood bath."   It was at an entertainment at the castle
given by the king that the first act of this
awful tragedy, called the *blood bath* in the annals of
Sweden, was performed. The archbishop, by previous
concert with the king, came before the throne, and demanded that Steckborg should be rebuilt, and the authors of his wrong should be punished. The accusation
being pointed against Sten Sturé and his adherents,
Christina Gillenstierna, in justification of her husband,
produced the deed which solemnly deposed the archbishop and decreed the destruction of his castle. This
was precisely what the king desired. He immediately
declared that he would treat all who had signed it as
heretics. They were asked separately whether they
acknowledged their signatures, and as they could not
deny them, they were all taken into custody, with the
exception of two bishops, who proved that they had
signed the document under compulsion. Thus, as subsequently in the case of the marriage festivities of
Henry of Navarre, the hall of feasting was suddenly
converted into a tribunal for the trial of alleged heretics and rebels.

The prisoners were committed for the night to the
tower of the chapel and other parts of the castle. A
tribunal, consisting of the archbishop and several
bishops and nobles was appointed by the king to
decide specifically upon the crime of which they were
guilty and to assign their punishment. The tribunal
declared that the prisoners were manifest heretics, according to the just law of the Holy Church, of the

Emperor and of Sweden. The punishment of heresy was death. Resistance to an archbishop in arms against the constituted authorities of the realm pronounced to be heresy! Nothing could be more absurd! But when a brutal tyrant like Christian is bent on getting rid of enemies one plea is as good as another. In this case no doubt Christian felt that it was better to direct the obloquy which would follow this wholesale murder, upon the church, rather than draw it directly upon himself, by resting it upon the much more plausible ground of treason.

The victims were immediately notified by their appointed executioner of their coming doom. They applied in vain for the last consolations of religion. On the following morning the question was proposed to them whether it was not heresy to confederate and conspire against the most Holy See of Rome. They were constrained to answer that it was, but contended that the punishment of a rebellious archbishop, could not be construed as conspiracy against the Pope. But their admission was feigned to be a confession of their guilt.

The execution of the nobles took place on November 8, just one week after the coronation. On the morning of that day the inhabitants of Stockholm were forbidden on pain of death to leave their houses, before a signal to be given by sound of trumpet. The cannons of the castle were loaded and others so placed as to command the principal streets. A heavy foreboding oppressed the minds of the citizens. When the clock struck twelve the trumpet sounded, and the people were summoned to the great square of the city. The castle gates were soon after opened, the drawbridge lowered, and the prisoners brought forth. There were Matthias, Bishop of Strengness, Vincentius, Bishop of Skara, and twelve secular nobles, most of them members of the State Council, including Eric Johnanson, the father of Gustavus, Joachim Brahe, whom his brother-in-law, Gustavus, had attempted to dissuade from going to the coronation, the burgomaster and town council of Stockholm, and many burgesses. A Danish knight, Nicholas Lyké, addressed the people, telling them not to be terrified at what they were about to witness; that the archbishop had three times on bended knees besought the king that the sentence of death should be executed upon the culprits, and that he had at length yielded to the request; but Bishop Vincentius interrupted him by exclaiming that there was not a word of truth in the statement; that the king could do nothing without lying and treachery, and he prayed God for vengeance on his tyranny. The incident shows the purpose of the king that the obloquy sure to follow this atrocious massacre should fall upon the Archbishop and the church.

Christian, who beheld these scenes from an open window of the old council house, now gave a sign that the execution should begin. Bishop Matthias was the first victim. He had taken with him to the coronation his chancellor Olaus Petri and Laurentius Petri his brother, who as the venerable bishop stood with his hands raised up to heaven, awaiting the blow of the executioner, rushed forward to embrace him. Before they could reach the spot his head rolled upon the ground. The two brothers could not restrain their indignation, and loudly proclaimed that it was an inhuman murder of a venerable and blameless man. They were seized and about to share the fate of their beloved bishop, but were spared when a German who had studied with them at Wittemberg declared that they were not Swedes. These two intrepid brothers became the chief agents of the Swedish Reformation.

Bishop Vincentius was next beheaded, then the lay nobles, then the burgesses. Olaus Magnus, who was unaccountably spared, says he saw ninety-four persons beheaded, and expected at each execution to be summoned next. When Eric Johnanson, the father of Gustavus, was led out for execution, a messenger from Christian came to him to offer him " pardon, grace and honor;" but the stout old patriot, thinking perhaps of his persecuted and fugitive son, refused to accept life from the blood-stained tyrant and cried out—"No, for God's sake let me die with these honest men, my brethren," and laid his head upon the block. Many were hanged or subjected to other horrible deaths. A contemporary historian, Zeigler, states that Johanness Magnus was crucified with circumstances of revolting cruelty. For three days, as new victims were enticed out of their hiding-places, by promises of pardon and security, the slaughter continued. Some were put to death because they could not restrain their tears at the loss of relatives and friends. No element of horror was absent from this carnival of blood. The retainers of the great nobles who had been executed were dragged from their horses as they attempted to escape from the city, and hanged in such numbers that girths and stirrup leathers, were used as substitutes for halters. A violent rain mingling with blood in the gutters of the streets, tinged everything with the hue of murder. For three days the slaughtered bodies remained in the market place; after which they were carried out to the South suburb of the city and burned. We must resort to the worst scenes of the

Reign of Terror in France, to find a parallel to this brutal slaughter.

Nor were these executions confined to Stockholm. They extended to Finland where Hemming Gadd suffered the just penalty of his defection from the cause to which he had given the best energies of his life, by laying his head upon the block at the age of eighty. The king's whole progress from Stockholm to Denmark was marked by cruel executions. Gibbets were erected in the market places and towns, previous to his arrival. At a monastery where he had ascertained that the abbot had hidden part of his stores in the woods, he ordered him and five monks to be thrown into a stream and drowned. And yet, even while the massacre was in progress in Stockholm, Christian had sent out a proclamation to the provinces, stating that " by the advice of the bishops, prelates, and other wise men, he had punished Sten Sture's confederates as heretics under the ban of the Church, but that he meant henceforth to govern the country mildly and peaceably according to the laws of S. Eric." More than six hundred of the highest and best citizens of Sweden had been slaughtered before the king left it in the beginning of the year 1521.

From the " History of the Revolution in Sweden, occasioned by the Change in Religion and the Alteration of the Government in that Kingdom," by the Abbé Vertot, and translated into English in 1729, I take the following account of the massacre. It is that of a Roman Catholic writer, but of one whose whole narrative shows him to have been honest and dispassionate. His book could scarcely have been satisfactory to the Papists.

After describing the method by which the Bishop of

Linkoping escaped the massacre, he thus continues his narrative: "Then they proceeded to the execution of the lay senators, beginning with Eric, the father of Gustavus. The consuls and magistrates of Stockholm and ninety-four lords who were arrested in the castle underwent the same fate. Yet the king instead of being satisfied with the death of so many illustrious persons, was extremely vexed that some lords whom he had particularly inserted in the black roll had escaped his fury. He imagined that they lay concealed in the town, and was so afraid that they would make their escape, and so desirous to arrest Gustavus, who he thought might be hid in some house in the city, that he gave full scope to his vengeance; he resolved to confound the innocent with the guilty, and to expose the town to the fury of the soldiers. As soon as they received those bloody orders, they fell upon the people who had come to be witnesses of that bloody spectacle, and promiscuously murdered all that had the misfortune to be in their way. Afterward they broke into the principal houses under the pretext of searching for Gustavus and the other proscribed lords. The citizens were stabbed in the arms of their shrieking wives, their houses were plundered and the honor of their wives and daughters was exposed to the brutish lust of the soldiers, who by orders, after the example of their inhuman sovereign, strove to out-do each other in the wildest and most extravagant barbarity.

"A certain gentleman of the Swedish nation was so sensibly touched by the moving sight of so many deplorable objects that he could not restrain the impetuosity of his grief, nor behold such scenes of horror without bewailing the misery of his country. The furious king was so enraged by these marks of compassion, which his guilty conscience interpreted as secret reproaches of his cruelty, that he commanded the unfortunate mourner to be fastened to a gibbet, his privy members were cut off, his belly ripped up, and his heart plucked out, as if pity and compassion had been the foulest of crimes.   Afterward the king pretending that the commiserator had rendered himself unworthy of Christian burial, by incurring the sentence of excommunication, ordered his body to be taken up and exposed in the public place among the mangled carcasses of his ancient friends.   He issued an order that no person should presume to bury any of these bodies on pain of death; and would have suffered them to lie in the open place, as a terrible monument of his vengeance, if the stench and putrefaction had not obliged him to command them to be taken away.   But before they were removed he could not forbear going on purpose to take a view of the dismal trophies of his fury.   At last he ordered them to be carried out of the city and be burned, that even death itself might not exempt them from a second punishment which he pretended to inflict upon them as excommunicated persons."   (Hist. p. 111-12.)

An historian of Sweden ends his record of these tragic events in these words: "While these horrors were being enacted, a noble youth wandering in the forests of Dalecarlia, fleeing before the emissaries of the tyrant, and hidden from his pursuers, sometimes in a rick of straw and sometimes under fallen trees, or in cellars and mines, was preserved by providence, whose great soul was already meditating the salvation of his country and eventually achieved it by the aid of God and Sweden's commonalty."

Christian's Character and Policy. Before the story of these wanderings is resumed, I pause to say a few words upon the character and policy of King Christian. It is not necessary to say, with the above facts before us, that he was one of the most base, crafty and cruel tyrants of whom history makes mention. But he belongs to a small and peculiar class of tyrants. He was one of those who entertained a deadly hatred of the aristocracy, not only from political jealousy, because of their constant attempts to limit his power, and to reach up to his level or to overtop him, but from a coarseness of nature and of manners, though born in the purple, which led him to choose his boon companions, and indulge his licentious passions among the lower classes. To this class belonged Ivan the Terrible of Russia, and Peter the Great, and I think I may add the first Napoleon. While, therefore, Christian showed himself fierce and cruel to the nobles and the cultivated classes, he was complaisant in his genial moods, to the common people, and secured the passage of many laws for their welfare and improvement. For, like Peter the Great of Russia, coarse in his tastes and endowed with great abilities, while he labored on the one hand to depress the nobility, he exerted himself on the other to develop the resources of his kingdoms, and to lift the laboring classes to a higher level of intelligence and prosperity. He caused good laws to be passed in favor of the commercial and laboring classes, and was the first king in northern Europe who opened schools for the poor of his dominions. He ordered the burghers of all the large cities in the three Scandinavian kingdoms, under the penalty of heavy fines, to compel their children to learn to read, and write and cipher. He also caused better books than were then in use to be prepared and printed for the public schools. He made the first attempt to establish a post in the country by forming a band of post runners, who, both in winter and summer, passed between Copenhagen and the chief towns of his dominions. Wayside inns were established at certain distances along the road, and the system was established, which still prevails in Norway, by which the local population were obliged to keep the roads in order and to supply relays of horses for travelers. He forbade bishops to burn witches, and to claim the old strand tax, or wreckage of stranded vessels. He put an end to selling peasants with the land. And strange it sounds to hear that the author of the blood bath of Stockholm was very much interested in the cultivation of flowers and vegetables, and by the advice of his queen sent for and employed Flemish gardeners. He would have proved in all probability a successful tyrant but for that passion of cruelty which led him to outrages too intolerable to remain unavenged, and that elaborate craft which is always short-sighted and sure ultimately to entrap its master in the toils which he weaves for others.

Wanderings and Dangers of Gustavus. After visiting his brother-in-law Joachin Brahe and his sister Margaret, Gustavus repaired to his father's estate of Ræfness and there lived some time concealed. He made himself known to the old Archbishop Jacob Ulfson, and learned from him that the peasants in Dalecarlia had risen against the government of Christian but had been defeated. The archbishop advised him to submit to the king, and informed him that his name was included in the amnesty which was proclaimed on the surrender of Stockholm. "Once," says

Geijer, "after such a conversation, when Jacob Ulfson had employed his eloquence in vain, it happened that an old servant of Joachin Brahe presented himself at the castle of Gripsholm, and rather by sighs and tears than words imparted the first tidings of the massacre at Stockholm." The terrible news was soon confirmed. The archbishop was dumb from horror and Gustavus prepared for flight.

He left Ræfness on horseback on the 26th of November, 1520, accompanied by a single servant who stole off with the saddle-bags, which contained all his effects and money. He chased the servant and secured the saddle-bags, but the thief escaped. When he reached the frontier of Dalecarlia, he assumed the dress of a peasant and served as he had opportunity as a farm laborer. When thus employed with Anders Pehrson, a rich miner at Rankhytta, a maid servant one day caught sight of a gold-embroidered collar beneath his jacket and informed her master of the fact. Looking attentively in his face, Pehrson recognized him as an old school fellow at Upsala; but while not disposed to betray him, he was unwilling to harbor a refugee so distinguished. The barn at which Gustavus threshed at Rankhytta is preserved as a state monument.* After breaking through the ice in passing over a ferry and spending the night shivering in a peasant's hut, he presented himself the next day to Arendt Pehrson who had served under him at Brankyrka, and did not scruple to discover himself to his old companion in arms. But

---

* King Charles XI. visited this barn in 1684. It is now marked with a monument of porphyry with this inscription: "Here worked as a thresher Gustavus Ericson pursued by foes of the realm but selected by providence to be the Saviour of the country. His descendant in the sixth generation, Gustavus III., raised this memorial."

Pehrson's fear of Christian was stronger than his sense of generosity and honor; and though he received Gustavus with seeming cordiality, he resolved to deliver him up to the king's lieutenant in the neighborhood. After Gustavus had retired for the night Pehrson left the house and returned early in the morning with the king's lieutenant and a body of thirty men to take him prisoner. But Gustavus had escaped through the kindness of Pehrson's wife. Suspecting the treachery of her lord from his absence, she warned her guest of his danger, provided him with a horse and sledge and guide and sent him to the Swedsjö parsonage. For this act she incurred the life-long enmity of her husband and won an honored name in the annals of Sweden. Gustavus remained about a week at the parsonage of Swedsjö, and when the worthy pastor could no longer protect him, he sent him secretly to Swen Elfson, a royal forester of great courage and presence of mind, living at Isala. Elfson's wife was no unworthy helpmate of such a husband. Some of the lieutenant's band came in search of her guest one day when she was making bread, and Gustavus was warming himself at the oven. His look indicated some disquiet and might have betrayed him had she not given him a smart blow with the ladle with which she was stirring the bread, and asked him with an expression of impatience whether he had never seen soldiers before, and sent him off to his duties in the barn.*

When he was obliged to shift his quarters again—the neighborhood being beset with Danish soldiers, and a persistent search made for him—Elfson sent him away hidden under some straw in a light wagon. Some

---

* This is the subject of one of the series of frescoes in the Cathedral of Upsala, which commemorates the most stiking incidents in the life of Gustavus.

Danish troopers coming up, in lieu of a more formal search, thrust their spears into the straw and wounded Gustavus. The blood began to trickle down on the snow, and would certainly have discovered his hiding place had not the quick-witted Elfson, by giving his horse unobserved a gash in the leg ·thus diverted attention from the point whence the blood issued.

Having thus eluded the troops by the dexterity of his guide, Gustavus arrived safe at Marness. Here he lay concealed under a large uprooted fir-tree, supplied with food by the peasants. From thence he penetrated farther into a forest and took up his abode upon a hill, still called the king's hill, which was surrounded by a morass, and again found a hiding-place under an old overturned fir-tree. On the green before the Church at Ratvic, his next retreat, he first publicly addressed the Dalesmen. As this incident leads to his probable reasons for leaving Dalecarlia, and points to the plan which he had devised for rousing his countrymen to resist the tyrant king, it may be well, before following him farther on his perilous adventures, to dwell for a few moments on the probable ground upon which he rested the hope that he might then commence and organize a patriotic crusade, which would ultimately drive the Danes from Sweden.

Dalecarlia and the Dalesmen. Dalecarlia—the land of dales—is a beautiful and fertile region of rich valleys, between high rugged mountains, beneath which lie inexhaustible mines of copper, iron and silver. The portion of it in the midst of which Upsala is situated is for many leagues a fertile and lovely plain, producing abundant crops and sustaining immense herds of cattle. The indefinite term Dalecarlia is applied also to the rugged regions which stretch to the North and the

West towards Norway, but historical Dalecarlia, and as it appears in the record of Gustavus, includes the two *Lans* or provinces of Westeras and Upsala, north and west of the province of Stockholm.

It has been already stated that Gustavus was induced to resort to Dalecarlia from his confidence in the independent character of the Dalesmen. But beyond this general confidence in the character of the people, there were historical traditions and advantages which would naturally lead him to hope that his appeal to them to rise and throw off the hated yoke of Christian would not be in vain. It was around Upsala and its immediate neighborhood that all the heroic national traditions, pagan and christian, gathered. Within one Swedish mile of that city was the old Upsala, the seat of the first god-king Odin, with his divine Aste, his council of gods, with his successors Njord and Freya, also gods; and there, descended from them, and inheriting the honor due to a divine parentage, reigned the first mortal king, Fiolner. There are the three vast mounds under which the first three kings Odin, Njord, and Freya, are believed to be buried, and at the foot of which for many centuries the kings of Sweden pronounced their oaths and received their consecration. It had been the right of the "upper" Swedes, inherited from the days of paganism, to dispose of the crown, a right which after the introduction of Christianity became the subject of many contests. It had been the custom for the Upland to nominate the king; and after his election and confirmation, the king set out upon his *cricksgeit*, in which he visited all the provinces, and received a formal recognition of him as their rightful lord. After the other provinces had vindicated their right to join in the election, the justiciaries, the authorized representatives of the provinces, gathered on the meadow of Mora, under the shadow of the mound of Odin. The mode of proceeding formally by the authority of the provinces in the election of the king, is thus described by Geijer:

"This assembly was called the Mora Thing. The justiciaries of the provinces were to repair thither, every one attended by twelve discreet and well-skilled men, with the assent of all the resident inhabitants of the circuit. The voices of these deputies and the law-man (justiciary) constituted the vote of the province. The justiciary of Upland voted first and then the rest in their order. Thereupon the king swore to the people on the book, with the holy relics in his hand, the oath embodied in the law, and lifting up his hand promised to God and the people to keep what he had sworn and by no means to break it, but rather to augment it by every good work, and especially by his royal word. In like manner the justiciaries and the people took their oath to the king, and by this were bound both young and old, the living and the yet unborn, the friend and the unfriend, the absent as well as the present. This was called *to swear by or at the Mora stone;* and an old record states that immediately after his election the king was raised upon the stone. It was then incumbent upon the king to ride in the manner before mentioned on his ericksgeit, or as it is called in the land law, 'to ride round the realm with the sun.'"

It was therefore no doubt not only because of the sturdy character of the Dalesmen that Gustavus betook himself to that region, but because he also felt that all the associations, traditions and habits of the people were such as would enable him to fire their hearts with a patriotic passion and ambition to redeem

their enslaved country. He could remind them that
it was the prerogative of Upland to cast the first vote
for the election of the king; and that Christian had
been imposed upon them without the formality of appealing to them for their consent. He could refer to
the long train of illustrious kings who had received
their consecration at the Mora stone; and this usurper
had entered into Stockholm by force of arms and the
slaughter of their countrymen, and sat there upon a
throne erected over a pool of the best and noblest
blood in Sweden. He might naturally have thought
that if he could receive their recognition as the champion whom they selected to commence the work of
the redemption of their country, such a designation
might wear something of the character, in the eyes of
his countrymen, of that old right of Upland to select
and elect a king, which the other provinces were merely
summoned to sanction, and which would lead to his
acceptance by the kingdom as its providentially and
historically designated leader and commander. That
such thoughts may have cheered and sustained the
hunted and heroic fugitive, appears in a high degree
probable from the fact that he determined to make his
first address to the Dalesmen in the Mora region and
near the Mora stone.

His Appeal to the Dales- men. The uprooted fir-tree which furnished his hiding place was not far from the Mora meadow.
At a moment when Ratvick seemed to be
free from the Danish troops who were tracking him,
Gustavus issued from his hiding-place and addressed
the people on the green before the church. He bade
the old to consider well, and the young to inform themselves, what a dreadful tyranny the Danes had introduced into Sweden; and how much they themselves

had suffered and ventured for the cause of their beloved country. He reminded them of the oppression
of Erickson, and of the heroic and successful resistance to it of Englebert. And now all Sweden was
again under the heel of the tyrant of Denmark, and its
noblest blood had been shed by him. His own father
"had chosen rather with his associates, the honor-lov-
ing nobles, to die than to be spared and survive them."
"If they would now save their land from slavery, he
would put himself at their head, and fight with them
for the freedom of the realm." This appeal did not
produce the impression which he had hoped for. The
full story of Christian's massacre had not yet penetrated the Dales. The peasants of Ratvick did not
personally know Gustavus, and his family was not
immediately associated with their history. They expressed their sympathy with him, but declined to com-
mit themselves to any action until they should have
consulted other parishes.

Still less encouraging was the result where he expected it would be the greatest, when he addressed the
peasants on the Mora meadow. To a large assembly
gathered there he gave a vivid description of the massacre at Stockholm, spoke of his own share in the ca-
lamity, and offered himself to be their leader "to avenge
the blood that had been spilt, and to teach the tyrant
that Swedes must be ruled by law, not ground down by
cruelty." We can readily imagine the patriotic ardor,
with which he must have made such an appeal. But
only a few of the peasants were in favor of arming at
once; the majority of them advised him to go further
into the woods, and informed him that he was sought
and tracked by many bands of Danish soldiers. Utterly discouraged by this reception, Gustavus again

sought still more distant and lonely hiding-places, and
at the close of the year crossed the boundary which
separates the eastern and western dales, intending to
take refuge in Norway. But soon a reaction took place
in the minds of this simple-hearted peasantry. The
story of this reaction should be told in no other words
than those of Sweden's great historian, Geijer. There
is a great charm in the beautiful simplicity of the
narrative, and a romantic interest in the events, in
that humble and narrow sphere, which determined the
civil and religious history of Sweden for the ensuing
centuries.

"Shortly after Gustavus quitted Ratvick several
Swedish nobles of the Danish faction arrived there for
the purpose of securing his person. Some peasants
who saw them coming in with about a hundred horses
on the ice of lake Silian, hastened to the church and
rang the bells. The wind blew towards the upper
country; a great concourse of people assembled as was
their wont on occasions of common peril, and the stran-
gers who had sought refuge partly in the priest's house,
and partly in the tower, which long after showed marks
of the Dalesmen's arrows, could only ransom their lives
by the assurance that they would do no harm to Gustavus.

"About the new year there arrived at Mora Lawrence
Olaverson, a captain of great experience in the service
of Sten Sturé the younger; and shortly after a nobleman of Upland named John Michelson. They drew
so lively a picture of the massacre of Stockholm that
the bystanders were affected to tears. The ericksgeit
of the king they said was at hand; his way would be
marked by the gallows and wheel; all the arms of the
Swedish peasants would be wrested from them and

consumed; and if their limbs were left to them unmutilated, a stick in the hand would be the only
weapon allowed them in the future; the imposition of
an additional tax for the maintenance of the new troops
was daily expected. The people murmured and complained that they had allowed Gustavus Erickson to
depart. In this their new guests told them they did
wrong; such a noble leader they stood much in need
of. Many a worthy Swedish warrior was now wandering like themselves, fugitives in the forest, who
would never submit to the dominion of the Danes, but
lead a free life so long as they might, until Sweden
should receive from God, a captain and a chief for
whom they would cheerfully put to hazard their life and
welfare." The Dalecarlians now sent off runners on
snow skates to seek out Gustavus day and night and
bring him back. They found him in the hamlet of Seln
in the upper part of the parish of Lima, whence he intended to seek a pathway across the mountains of
Norway.

He returned in their company to Mora, where the
principal and most influential yeomen of all the parishes
in the eastern and western dales elected him to be
" Lord and chieftain over them and the command of the
realm of Sweden." Some scholars who had arrived from
Westeras brought with them new accounts of the tyranny of Christian. Gustavus placed these students in
the midst of a circle of the peasants to tell their story
and answer the questions of the crowd. Old men represented it as a comfortable sign for the people that as
often as Gustavus discoursed to them the north wind
always blew, which was an old token to them that God
would grant them a good success. Sixteen active
peasants were appointed to be his body guard; and

two hundred young men were called his foot-goers.
The chronicles reckon his reign from this small beginning; while the Danes and their abettors in Stockholm
long after continued to speak of him and his party as a
band of robbers in the woods.

It would be interesting, if our limits allowed, to
trace the gradual development of this band of peasants
into a well-organized army under the skillful hand of
Gustavus, and to follow the successive steps by which
he gained the confidence and the enthusiastic affection
and admiration of his countrymen, and reached a
position of commanding influence and power. He at
once displayed all the qualities of a great commander
and administrator. In the beginning of February, he
marched to the great copper mine, took its superintendent prisoner, seized upon all the king's and the
Danish property in the place, and made his first ban-
ners from the silks that were captured. Soon after he
returned to that place with 1,500 men, and from that
time great and rapid accessions to his ranks took place.
The king's troops were sent out to meet him, but were
beaten and driven back. As Gustavus passed into
Westmanland, the people flocked to his standard; and
when on S. George's day, the 23rd of April, he organized and reviewed his army, it was found to be 15,000
strong. At this point of his progress, he issued a formal proclamation of war against Christian. In it he
declared that Christian had not lawfully been elected
king; if he had been, he had forfeited his throne by his
atrocious tyranny and his violation of the laws of Sweden;
and he proudly referred to the fact that he had never
sworn allegiance to him, and that he took up arms
against him without violating a plighted faith. This
last fact gave him a prodigious influence with his coun-

trymen. They gathered about him under the influence of patriotic passion and personal devotion which enabled him, after two years of varied successes and reverses, to enter Stockholm in triumph on the 21st of June, 1523.

The Execution of Slaghec. After the massacre of Stockholm and the departure of Christian to Denmark, the Bishops Slaghec and Beldnaké were appointed administrators of the kingdom in his absence. But Slaghec soon left Sweden, having been advanced to the Archbishopric of Lund, the primacy of the Danish Church. But he did not long enjoy the honors of that envied station—the highest to which a northern ecclesiastic could be raised. On the first news of the massacre at Stockholm, Johannes Magnus, Canon of Linkoping, and afterwards Archbishop of Upsala, had hastened to Rome to demand vengeance against Christian. The execution of two Bishops so aggravated the enormity of that crime in the eyes of the Pope that, though unwilling to strike the king on account of the emperor, he would not refuse inquiry. M. D. Potentia, a Neapolitan monk was dispatched for the purpose with secret orders to view the matter in a light as favorable as possible for the king; while Christian, advised of his danger and determined to save himself, resolved to sacrifice Archbishop Slaghec, in order that he might be personally exculpated.

Slaghec had been in the possession of his dignity but two months when he was summoned to Copenhagen to answer to the charge of having been the instigator of the massacre. The charge was readily proved. He was found guilty and sentenced to death. On the 22nd of June, 1522, the sentence was executed. The king had left Copenhagen, and given orders that

the execution should take place during his absence.
The scene of it was the old Market-place or Square of
the city. A gallows was erected and a pile of fagots
heaped up near the Council House, and here in his rich
robes, the guilty tool and victim of the guiltier king
was conducted. Inasmuch as his was the double crime
of treason against the State and of spiritual treason
against the Vicar of Christ, in executing two of his
spiritual servants, he was forced up towards the gallows, as if to suffer upon it, and then led to the blaz-
ing pile, where, with no sympathy from the crowd, he
was burned.

The proceed-
ings and De-
thronement
of Chris-
tian. While Gustavus was making progress in the
North, Christian was pursuing those harsh
and cruel measures which were well calculated to hasten his overthrow. He had caused
the mothers and wives and children of the most distinguished Barons of Stockholm to be conveyed to Denmark. Among these were the mother and the two
sisters of Gustavus, whom Christian, in spite of the remonstrances and entreaties of his wife, threw into a
dungeon. Here they perished, and as it was believed
and charged by Gustavus, by violence. Christian also
issued an order to his generals and officials to put to
death all Swedes of distinction who should fall into
their hands. A massacre similar to that at Stockholm,
though not on so extensive a scale, only for want of
sufficient victims, was by his direction perpetrated at
Abo, the capital of Finland.

After leaving Sweden to be thus harried and oppressed, Christian made a visit with much splendor to
his brother-in-law, Charles V., in the Netherlands, to
secure the dowry of his Queen, and to solicit his aid
in a war against Duke Frederic of Holstein. The ob-

ject which he had in view seemed definite, but the means which he employed were various and contradictory, and such as would inevitably bring about failure and defeat. He aimed to depress the power of the nobility and clergy; to elevate and gratify and govern through the burghers and peasants; to destroy the ascendency of the Hanse towns, and to annex Holstein, and so utterly to crush and terrify Sweden as that it should lie henceforth passive under his sway. But his measures were fitful, incoherent and inconsistent. He seemed mastered by a feverish restlessness, which led him into projects and policies which crossed and nullified each other and led to his ultimate ruin. He made the Papal bull the pretext for his cruelty in Sweden, and yet on his return to Denmark instituted measures for the introduction of the Reformation into that kingdom. He even opened a correspondence with Luther, and invited Carlstadt to Copenhagen; and when investigation into the massacre of Stockholm was threatened, made application to the Pope for the canonization of Scandinavian saints. He raised the infamous Slaghec to the Archbishopric of Lund, and afterward, as we have seen, threw upon him the responsibility of the massacre of Stockholm and consigned him to the stake.

One year after the execution of Slaghec, when Christian was levying a new tax upon the kingdom for the prosecution of the unpopular war against Holstein, the dissatisfaction of the kingdom came to a head, and the nobles in council at Viborg, on the 20th of January, 1523, drew up a deed of renunciation of his authority, and declared that they had chosen Frederic, his uncle, Duke of Holstein, to fill the vacant throne. This act of renunciation enumerated his crimes and his atrocious tyranny, and declared that obedience to his intolerable rule had ceased to be a duty. The craven and abject spirit in which the king pleaded to be allowed a further trial, and threw the blame of his maladministration upon his advisers, and promised the most absolute conformity thereafter to the will of the council, exhibits that cowardly nature which so often leads to cruelty. Although the powerful province of Sealand and the nobles of Scania took an oath of fidelity to the king, he did not dare to trust them, or even to rely upon his army. He collected twenty ships in which he placed the public records, the treasures and the crown jewels and his wife and child. The evil genius of the king, Sigbert, the mother of one of his mistresses, who had either prompted or approved of all his cruelties, and exercised a most sinister influence over him, was conveyed to a ship in a chest, that she might escape the vengeance of the people, by whom she was vehemently abhorred. Thus ended the dreadful reign of Christian II. in Denmark and Sweden.

It may be well to follow the fortunes of Christian to their wretched end. He first fled to Holland, and remained there several years. In 1531, he landed in Norway with an army of Dutch and Germans, and was well received by the inhabitants. But the treaty made by Frederic with Sweden and Lubeck, enabled him to overthrow the army of Christian and to take him prisoner. Contrary to the pledge of his uncle's commander, who had promised him freedom, Christian was carried to Sonderberg in the lonely island of Als, and thrown into a dark dungeon below the tower. In that wretched prison in which light and air could penetrate only through a small grated window, which served at the same time for the transmission of the scanty food furnished him, Christian spent seventeen years of his life, with a half-witted and deformed Norwegian dwarf for his attendant and sole companion. A striking modern picture of Christian and his companion in prison, in the picture gallery of the palace at Copenhagen, leaves an ineffaceable impression upon the mind of the beholder.

On the death of Frederic I., his son, Christian III., wished that he might be released, on the pledge that he would retire to Germany and make no more efforts to recover the throne. But the Danish nobles were quite unwilling to rely upon his pledges, and all the relief that Christian III. could obtain for him was a removal to the Kallunberg castle, where he was permitted to' pass the last ten years of his life in comparative comfort, and where he died in 1559, within a few months of his namesake, Christian III.

Gustavus becomes Regent, Aug. 24, 1521. After the capture of Westeras and an unsuccessful attack upon Upsala, a convocation of the partisans of Gustavus, which claimed to represent the States of Sweden, took place at Wadstena on the 24th of August, 1521. There were present sixty nobles and many representatives of the burghers and the clergy. It was here, at a critical crisis of his life, that Gustavus made one of those speeches which turned the doubtful balance of events decidedly in his favor. A brief summary of it has been preserved, sufficient to suggest how stirring must have been such an appeal, from one whose heroic resistance to the tyrant, and whose romantic adventures and splendid personality must have vividly impressed the hearts and the imaginations of a people whom indignation had rendered ready for self-sacrifice and suffering. He told them that there were but two courses for them to pursue: "If they were content to be forever slaves to the Dane, and to abandon their possessions to the avarice of a greedy neighbor; if they had hearts to see the remaining flower of their nobility cut off, and could endure that Sweden, which had not only supported its own independence, but had given the law to other lands, should degenerate into a Danish province—then, indeed, they had only to sit down quietly and watch the footsteps of the tyrant. But if they loved freedom—if they would avenge the innocent blood that had run so piteously in their streets—if their houses and possessions were dear to them—if they would prove themselves worthy sons of their renowned fathers, then they would take the sword, and not let it sleep until they had dethroned the tyrant and regained the crown which he had wrested from their hands. Circumstances were most favorable to their enterprise. Christian was hated by his own people, and all his attention was required to secure himself in his hereditary dominions. He—Gustavus—had already, with the help of the Dalesmen, subdued a large portion of the realm, and the chief fortresses were now so hard beset that they could not offer a long resistance. The victory would soon be complete if they would only combine their councils and unite their strength."

The appeal was decisive. The estates immediately offered the crown to Gustavus. "That was the only way," they said, "to repay him for his services, and to save the kingdom." But Gustavus had the prudence and the foresight which made him see that his influence at that stage of his progress would be greater if he declined the crown and accepted a regency, which would in effect be kingship in all but the name. He replied that "he had taken up arms from zeal and compassion

for the people. The name of king had already, from
the abuse of it, begun to have a hateful sound. They
should unite their strength, and first place themselves
in a condition to choose a native Swedish king. Then
whomsoever they should deem fit for the honor, to him
he would show all loyalty and obedience."

Gustavus proclaimed King, June 17, 1523. From this period the military successes of
Gustavus became more decided. After two
years of siege, Stockholm surrendered. Just
previous to that event, June 7, 1523, a State
Council assembled at Strengness, when the newly
elected Archbishop, Knut, suggested that it was now
necessary to choose a king, since Christian had ceased
to be king even of Denmark. All the Council with
one voice declared for Gustavus. "He received their
congratulations with a grave countenance, thanked
his countrymen for their love and confidence, and said
that his services did not merit so great a reward, and
that he was weary of the burden and anxieties he had
already undergone. He begged them to choose one
of the old knights and nobles then present, and he
would give him his truth and allegiance." Tears and
exclamations and remonstrances interrupted his address. It is a curious fact, in connection with the part
which he subsequently took and was then prepared to
take in the Reformation of Sweden, that he at last
consented to accept the crown upon the pressing
instances of the Papal Legate.

Frederic I. of Denmark wrote to the estates of
Sweden that in accordance with the stipulations of the
treaty of Calmar, he should be acknowledged King of
Sweden. They replied that they had already elected
Gustavus Erickson to be Sweden's king. Thus was
the union of the treaty of Calmar dissolved, after it

had lasted 126 years. Previous to the surrender of Stockholm, the armies of Gustavus had been success- ful in expelling the Danes from the southern part of Sweden. On midsummer eve, the 21st of June, Gus- tavus made his entrance into Stockholm. Before the end of the year, Finland was brought into obedience.

The country was thus freed from foreign enemies, but it was full of the elements of discord and dissat- isfaction. That, in the circumstances under which Gustavus ascended the throne, he was able to main- tain his position, to pacify the kingdom, and develop its resources, and above all, that without any popular movement towards the Reformation, he was able to establish it by virtue of his overmastering character and against immense obstacles, without and within his kingdom, justly entitles him to the place which has been assigned him, by all who have studied his career, as one of the greatest men in the whole com- pass of European history.

CHAPTER III.

THE enthusiasm with which the Estates sanctioned the proposition of Canute, the Provost of the Cathedral of Westeras, that Gustavus should be elected king, might have animated him to accept an office, the enormous difficulties of which he could not but have foreseen, but which his patriotic love of country would not allow him to evade. Even if he had contemplated the task with passionate repugnance, he could not have found it in his heart to decline a position which his own agency had made it necessary that some one should fill, and which he must have known could not have been filled so worthily and efficiently by any one as by himself. It is not often that a crown has been pressed upon any one with such genuine and affectionate importunity. The following is the account of this remarkable scene given by Vertot:

" The speaker of the Estates (Provost Canute) represented to the Assembly the absolute necessity of proceeding speedily to the election of a king. Then he employed all his art in painting forth the qualities of an excellent Prince, one that was vigilant, laborious, full of courage, and endowed with a sufficient stock of valor and prudence to oppose the unjust pre-

tensions of the Danes to the Swedish crown: that in
this description they might see and take notice of the
picture of Gustavus. He concluded that after all the
services which the Administrator had done to the
State, and the illustrious proofs he had given of his
extraordinary endowments and virtues, they were
obliged, in gratitude to him, and in justice to the interests of those they represented, to confer the royal
title and authority upon their benefactor.

"This discourse was received with an universal
applause. The nobility and commons, transported
with their zeal and affection, prevented the senators
and deputies. The whole assembly proclaimed with
a loud voice, 'Gustavus, King of Sweden!' It was
impossible to gather the votes, or to proceed according to the usual forms observed in such cases. His
praises were echoed through the whole convention;
he was styled the savior and deliverer of his country.
The peasants and burghers, mingling confusedly with
the deputies, neglecting all marks of distinction, and
even forgetting the respect they owed to the senators
and other lords, struggled and crowded to approach
the king. The name of Gustavus was repeated by
every mouth; he was the object of every eye; and all
in general endeavored to express their joy at his election, and to congratulate their own happiness in having an opportunity to contribute to his advancement."

Difficulties of the King's Position. The town of Strengness was itself a proof
of one of the enormous difficulties—*the des-
olation of the country*—which he was called
upon immediately to confront. It had become almost
a ruin through the ravages of civil war. This condition of the town, suggestive of that of the whole
country, had impressed the council with the convic-

tion that there was no choice but between utter
national ruin, and the overthrow of the tyranny of
Christian. This conviction was deepened when Gustavus made his public entry into Stockholm. Half of
the houses were empty; and of the population of the
city on the accession of Christian only one fourth remained. To fill up the gap the king invited the
citizens of other towns to settle there, and offered
them great inducements to do so. This invitation
he was compelled to renew twelve years after, "seeing," he said, "that Stockholm had not revived from
the days of King Christian." And these were specimens of the condition of most of the towns and rural
estates of the lower and more populous portion of the
kingdom.

The power of the great lords was another obstacle
in the way of the speedy settlement of the kingdom.
One effect of the union of Sweden to Denmark had
been greatly to increase their influence. According
to the terms of the union, the Council, in the absence
of the king, governed the kingdom. As members of
the Council, the great nobles who composed it had constant opportunities to increase their exclusive privileges, to enlarge their estates, and to become more
independent of the supreme but distant authority of
the king. Many of the crown fiefs had been appropriated by them to their own use, and were thus in the
inevitable process of passing into their permanent possession. Many of the difficulties of the king arose from
this source. With characteristic foresight he saw that
this contest with the nobles for the recovery of the
crown and church lands would at once arise; and accordingly he availed himself of the first enthusiasm
created by his wonderful success to propose to the

Council " whether he might not freely dispose of the crown fiefs, as the law book declares, without ill will?" During the union, and especially during the long absence of King John, the kingdom seemed about to be parcelled out into principalities, under a few of the great magnates who were most powerful in the Council. This state of things it was impossible for the king immediately to change. The General Council at Stockholm had constituted branches in the various provinces, in which some members of the Central Council sat and exercised a predominant influence. Thus Gustavus found himself at once confronted with an oligarchy which had spread a net-work of influence and of organization over all the kingdom, and the members of which had possessed themselves of a large portion of the Royal domains. These it was necessary to recover without exciting to revolt the powerful lords, whose loyalty was the condition of continued possession of the throne. It was an immense difficulty. How wisely, by personal influence, by intimidation, and by the stern exercise of power, where it was called for, he so far overcame it as to recover most of the crown lands, and to become, not the mere agent of the great lords, but their master, we shall see in the progress of the history.

The turbulent independence of the people caused the king in the commencement of his reign frequent and most vexatious difficulties. The circumstances in which the people had been called to intervene in opposition to the Danish kings, had made them exacting and turbulent and difficult to satisfy. This was especially the case with the Dalesmen. At the call of Englebert they had expelled the tyrant Ericson, and made their leader Regent of the kingdom. From that period,

proud of their success, they had put forth many pretensions. The native Regents, Englebert, and the
three successive Sturés, and the one native king,
Charles Canutson, were compelled to profess to depend wholly on their support. In order to protect
themselves from rival aspirants to their office, they
found it necessary to flatter and conciliate the people,
by acknowledging their dependence on them, and by
conformity to their democratic tastes and habits. The
threatened partition of the kingdom among the great
lords led to a counter-development and manifestation
of popular power. During the troubled times, when
the Danish government was powerless, the people in
the provinces often assumed self-government, took up
arms and formed alliances when they were dissatisfied
with the local lords or authorities placed over them by
the Regent. This was the case more frequently in
upper than in lower Sweden. Hence, in consequence
of the immense services which the Dalecarlians, and
Northern Sweden generally, had rendered to Gustavus, he found them subsequently insubordinate, clam-
orous for special privileges, and unwilling to bear
their proportionate burdens of taxation and of military service.

The influence of the Church too was decidedly adverse
to the person and policy of the king. The Church was
in fact a foreign power established in the kingdom,
rather than a constituent part of it. Its great dignitaries
had generally been partisans of the Union; because they
received their appointments from the Pope, through
the influence or dictation of the Danish crown. The
lower clergy, dependent on their superiors, assumed
the same position. They had always been obnoxious
to the patriotic party. Englebert was violently hostile

to the Bishops; and the three Regents Sturé were constantly involved in contests with them. The execrated
Archbishop Trollé opened the way for the tyrant Christian to the throne. In the war which ensued the exasperation against the bishops, the clergy and the
monks found expression in many acts of violence.
Their great riches furnished a tempting resource to
Gustavus to supply the needs of his army; and the licentiousness of the priests and monks seemed to him
to condone reprisals for the outrages which the nation
had for centuries endured without redress.

But the most immediately pressing of all the difficulties of the king were *financial*. He had been compelled to borrow money and secure ships and men and
materials from Lubeck to carry on the war. That sharp
commercial town pressed him hard and over-promptly
for payment. On the very day of his election as king,
a deputation from Lubeck demanded an immediate
liquidation of his debt to the city. He requested an
extension of the time. This was granted only on hard
conditions, for he had distinctly pledged himself for
the payment so soon as the government should be de-
finitely settled. He was compelled to agree that Sweden
should conclude no treaty with Christian or any other
power without the consent of Lubeck; that on the surrender of Stockholm and Calmar, all goods found in
them which the Lubeck and Dantzic merchants should
claim upon oath as theirs, because not paid for, should
be restored to them; and that the wares of the same
cities should be admitted free of duty; and that the
whole foreign trade of Sweden should be confined to
the Hanse towns. It was a most ungenerous advantage
taken of the embarrassing circumstances in which the
king was placed; and the demand that the government

should be made responsible—for that in effect it was
—for the unfulfilled obligations of private merchants,
was unprecedented and grossly unjust. But the king
was not in a position openly to resist these demands.
In an address and appeal to the people, Gustavus stated
the urgent necessities of his position, with a view no
doubt to prepare them for and to vindicate in advance
the radical measure which he was about to adopt. It
is an indication of his personal feeling towards the
Church, that he did not hesitate to lay his hands upon
that portion of her wealth which was regarded as most
sacred, and the appropriation of which to secular purposes would be considered by the devout children of
the Church, not robbery only, but the grossest sacrilege.
The Church was in possession of two thirds of the landed
property of the kingdom; but as that could not be made
immediately available for his urgent needs, he resolved
to appropriate the sacred vessels used in the public
services, and the reliquaries, and the gold and gems,
the gifts of kings and nobles, in the treasuries of churches
and of convents. It is a striking proof of the realized
absolute necessity of his government to their national
existence, that such a measure could have been carried
out without a revolt upon the part of the people, who
had thus far shown no desire to throw off the Roman
yoke. It seems scarcely credible that in the then condition of the public conscience, the following demands
could have been obeyed: "We therefore enjoin you,"
says this document in the address to the clergy and
the commissions appointed to carry out the royal will,
"without delay to search in your churches and monasteries, both in towns and in the adjoining country, and
observe what can best be spared and select from the
valuables—to wit, the *monstrances*, the *chalices*, or what-

ever else of the kind there may be, and also any coin
which may come to hand, and send them here by a sure
messenger, without delay or negligence. When we receive the same, and know the amount, we will give an
acknowledgment, so that the debt shall be duly paid
when the state shall be in better circumstances." But
all the devices of the king to raise revenue during the
early part of his reign did not suffice to meet the wants
of the Government. He was thwarted in many of his
plans and defeated in many efforts to bring his kingdom into peace and order, for the want of money.
None but a man of commanding ability and fertile in
resources, and with a strong hold upon the affection
and confidence of his people, could have worked his
way through and over the enormous difficulties which
beset his path.

Last and not least of the difficulties with which
Gustavus was called to struggle was *the distrust ana
opposition of the priesthood.* We have seen that the
priesthood, high and low, were partisans of the Danish
rule. This alone would have sufficed to have made
them the king's secret foes. But when he laid his hands
upon the sacred vessels and silve shrines and lamps,
the golden crucifixes and the gem-encrusted caskets of
holy relics, this distrust passed into thinly veiled and
holy horror. While it could have been scarcely possible that the growing alienation of the mind of the king
should have been wholly disguised, he yet abstained,
during the first two years of his reign, from any open
opposition to the doctrine or discipline of the Church;
although he did not altogether escape some personal
collisions with its administrators. It was, as we shall
see, one of the main problems which he was called to
solve, to prepare the way gradually for the abolition of

- the Papacy and yet to do this so cautiously as not to
create a rebellion, which in the early part of his reign,
before his power was consolidated, he might have been
unable to overcome. His position in this respect was
not unlike that of Queen Elizabeth, and his cautious
policy was quite the counterpart of hers. But on her
side there were two great advantages which were wanting to Gustavus. She was the recognized lawful heir to
the throne, in a country where the principle of royal hereditary right was a religious dogma, and where the
Protestant principles which she aimed to introduce and
establish, were already fervently held by a large and
intelligent portion of the people. Gustavus on the
contrary was an elected king, and the principles of the
Reformation had made no progress and were scarcely
known to exist when he ascended the throne.

The Intro- The Lutheran doctrines had been introduced
duction of secretly into Sweden by Olaus and Laurentius
Lutheran-
ism into Petri a few years before Gustavus was pro-
Sweden. claimed king. They were native Swedes,
the sons of a smith at Orebo, and they had studied
with great distinction under Luther and Melancthon,
and had been encou. ged by them to return and labor
to evangelize their native land. They were learned
and intrepid men, who were animated with holy zeal,
tempered by discretion. In 1520 Olaus was made a
Canon of Strengness and in secret preached against indulgences, vows of celibacy, the worship of saints and
images, prayers for the dead, auricular confession and
the power of the Pope. The shameless traffic in indulgences, which prevailed in Germany and Switzerland,
and which aroused the opposition of Luther and Zwingli,
also stimulated the zeal of the brothers Petri, to a more
open denunciation of the Papal claims. During the aw-

ful scenes which occurred while Christian II. had possession of the kingdom, and the war which followed,
the preaching of the Petri attracted but little attention.
But while these events prevented a wide dissemination
of their doctrines, they at the same time allowed them
to labor unmolested. The king, who had corresponded
with Luther in 1524, advanced Olaus to the Rectorship
of the Church in Stockholm, and appointed his brother
Laurentius a professor in the University of Upsala. At
this time the king had become a firm but unavowed
believer in the doctrines of Luther. After the close of
the war the preaching of the two brothers, from the
vantage-ground of their high position, began to attract
much attention. As it now met with violent opposition
Gustavus appointed a discussion of the points in dispute
to be held in his presence. The result was, as the king
had foreseen, favorable to the Reformers. In consequence of this discussion twelve questions were prepared
for examination in an assembly of divines to be appointed by the king.

A conference of Lutheran and Roman Divines. These questions were examined in a conference held at Upsala at Christmas, 1524.
Olaus Petri, in the presence of the king,
challenged the Canons of Upsala to defend
the doctrines of the Roman Church. At first the
Chapter declined to engage in the controversy, but
finally appointed Peter Gallé as their champion. The
questions submitted involved the chief topics in controversy between the Lutheran and the Roman Church.
They were as follows: "Whether God's Word is the
sole rule of faith; what are the limits of Church authority; whether the supremacy of the Pope and his agents
be for Christ or against Him; whether man can be
saved by his own works and deservings or otherwise

than by God's grace and mercy; whether men have a right to order the administration of the Lord's Supper in a way different from Christ's institution; whether there is any scriptural warrant for the doctrine of purgatory; and lastly, whether the Saints are to be worshiped and prayed to, and are our protectors, patrons, mediators and intercessors before God."

A sharp discussion followed, in which Peter Gallé relied upon the Fathers, and Olaus on the Scriptures alone. After it had continued some time, it was stopped by the king at a point where it was becoming violent, and would have been likely to have ended in commotion and confusion. He requested the disputants to reduce their arguments to writing, that they might be considered more fully in a larger conference or synod of the clergy.. These productions were printed and circulated through the kingdom, and prepared the way in the more remote portions of the country for the reception of the Reformed faith. But the most effective publication on the Protestant side was that of the Bible translated into Swedish by Chancellor Lars Anderson at the king's command. This was issued in the following year.   ,

The manifold complications of the king made it impossible that he should yet appear as the apologist or champion of the Reformation. It was evidence of great moral force on his part, that he resolutely protected the Reformers, and refused to allow them to be persecuted or silenced. The Bishop of Linköping urged the king not to shield those who promulgated the new heresy, and to prohibit the sale of Luther's writings. The king replied that he was bound to protect every one of his subjects until they should be convicted of some crime or civil offense. Thus early did he announce the noble principle, unfortunately not adopted by all the Reformers, from which he never subsequently swerved, that religious opinions when they did not pass into, or were not made the plea for crimes against the State or against the laws, should not be punished by the government. To the demand which was made that he should prohibit the sale of Luther's books he gave the following firm and calm reply: " As to the request that we should forbid the purchase of Luther's books, we do not see how we can grant it until we hear them condemned by impartial judges, especially since books against Luther are brought into the country. It seems, therefore, according to our poor understanding that there should be an opportunity of reading the one as well as the other." Under the circumstances in which he was placed it was a brave and direct reply, when mere policy, uninfluenced by conscience, would have led to evasion or equivocation.

The War of Gustavus against Severin Norby. For in addition to those general and permanent difficulties of which we have spoken, Gustavus was at that time engaged in a struggle against Severin Norby, a partisan of Christian, who had taken possession of the island of Gothland in the name of the dethroned king, and exercised there a very independent sway. Norby was a brilliant sailor and soldier of fortune, who combined the characteristics of the old Vikings, of the Italian *condottieri* of the middle ages, and of those contemporary knights in Germany, who, like Ulrich Von Hutten and Sickengen, were accomplished scholars. The powerful little capital of Gothland—Wisby—was one of the rich Hanse towns of the middle ages, the rival and the peer of prosperous Lubeck. It was surrounded by powerful walls, which were fortified by massive and lofty towers, and within it was an abode of wealth and a hive of industry. Its present dilapidated condition still attests its former greatness; for its walls and towers remain, and within the circuit of a mile are the ruins of a dozen churches, some of them having almost the solidity and size, and elaborate architecture of cathedrals, in which the merchants and citizens of various nationalities and tongues were accustomed to worship. But as its commercial prosperity declined and its population diminished, its large shipping and its impoverished citizens were often employed in piratical adventures. This island with its fortified position and its piratical reputation furnished an asylum and a base of operations, precisely suited to the character and purposes of Norby. At an early period it had been colonized by Sweden, was converted to Christianity by S. Olaf, in his own peculiar militant style of missionary zeal, and had acknowledged allegiance and paid tribute to the parent state. The Swedish historian Geijer traces the rise of the Hanseatic League to this prosperous commercial community; and it was not until after the middle of the fourteenth century, 1361, that, in conflict with the greatly superior power of Denmark, it received the fatal blow from which it never rallied.

When therefore Norby took possession of the island he was at once welcomed by its inhabitants as its lord. He proceeded to enlarge those piratical enterprises to which they looked for their prosperity; and he enriched the impoverished city by unlading all the booty from the ships which he captured; and then, sending them away empty, he wished them a good voyage and a happy return, with fresh and fuller cargoes. He even issued coins, as an independent prince, with his own

name on the one side, and the arms of Gothland—
most inappropriate to its then position—a lamb with a
standard on the other! The life of a sea rover at this
time in the Baltic, notwithstanding laws against it,
instead of covering those who practiced it with infamy,
seems to have invested them with a glamor of romantic
adventure, something like that which invested the
Vikings of old, especially when, as in the case of
Norby, it was professedly adopted from loyalty to a
deposed and lawful sovereign.

Gustavus was made to feel that he could not have
secure possession of his throne so long as Norby and
his little kingdom furnished a rallying point and a
nucleus for all the remaining opposition to his reign.
Moreover there was good reason to believe that the
aspiring adventurer aimed at dispossessing Gustavus
and obtaining the regency of the kingdom by a marriage with the widow of the late administrator, Christina
Gyllenstierna. Her own conduct and language gave
countenance to this belief. When a rumor to that effect
was spread among the Dalesmen to excite them to
revolt, and when Gustavus, in order to defeat such a
scheme, proposed—what was equivalent to a command
—that she should be united to Jno. Tureson, the son
of the high steward, she gave an explanation of her
relation to Norby, which the king affected to accept.
"She was afraid," she said, "that Norby had given out
the year before that she was betrothed to him, and that
he held her written engagement. But he could not
prove that she had plighted her faith either to himself
or to any other man since the death of her husband.
She had written to him but once, and then told him
that she was not disposed again to marry; but if she
were inclined he would be the man of her choice. Now

she did not know whether he had so understood these words, as though she had meant to take him for her wedded lord; if he had, he was mistaken. True, she had sent him a gold ring and tablet; but this was only to testify the sense she entertained of the courteous attention he had paid her when she was captive in Denmark." Skillful words certainly, but not such as could exonerate her from disloyalty to her own king, in maintaining such close and friendly relations with his avowed and open enemy!

It was with no little reluctance that Gustavus entered upon the task of capturing Wisby and destroying the power of Norby. He no doubt felt that, even if his throne was not endangered, his prestige would be undermined, and his influence lessened, so long as a powerful enemy could keep the field against him. An expensive expedition which strained the resources of the king, was sent to Gothland and took possession of all the island except Wisby; and after his unsuccessful siege, the capital was finally surrendered to the Danish king. Gustavus was chagrined and dissatisfied with this result, and resolved never again to engage in any enterprise outside of his own dominions; but his last formidable and active enemy was now out of his way, and he hoped to be able to give his undivided attention to the welfare of Sweden, and to the promotion of the Reformation.*

* The remainder of Norby's adventurous and tumultuous life was in keeping with that which we have described above. He escaped with a remnant of his fleet from Gothland, endeavored in vain to enlist Frederic of Denmark in a war with Gustavus, proceeded to Russia to exasperate the Czar against both Sweden and Denmark, and, failing in that effort, was imprisoned in Moscow for three years. Liberated at the intercession of the Emperor, he entered into his service, and was killed at the siege of Florence, in 1530. That his piratical career enhanced rather than diminished his fame appears

Commotions Caused by Anabaptists. Everywhere we see the Reformation at its rise discredited and hindered by the extravagances of the Anabaptists. It was so in Germany and Bohemia. The same little group of Anabaptist leaders appear in succession in Wittemberg and in Stockholm. It was in the same year, 1524, in which the discussion took place before Gustavus that Melchior Rink, a furrier, and Knipperdoling, both from Munster, arrived in Stockholm. They soon met with supporters, and obtained possession of the principal churches, where they preached from the Book of Revelation on the reign of the Saints in the Millennium, which was soon to come. Their converts and partisans, excited to a high pitch of enthusiasm, broke into churches and convents, destroyed the images, organs and ornaments, which they found there, and threw the fragments into the streets and market-places. Olaus Petri's ineffectual efforts to quell the disturbances did not save him from the sharp rebukes of Gustavus. Some of the authors of these disturbances were imprisoned, and some banished from the kingdom, and forbidden to return. But the affair gave great scandal, and created fresh prejudices against the Lutheran doctrines. This was increased in some of the provinces by the Antinomian doctrines and the loose lives of preachers who had been infected with Anabaptist opinions. Gustavus met this difficulty with his usual skill and firm-

from an eulogistic Latin poem to his memory by the former Vice-Chancellor to Christian II., which ends thus:

.   "That life which Moscow's dungeons could not quell,
        Nor Neptune quench amid his boundless swell,
        In Latium sunk, the citadel of fame,
        That through the world might spread so great a name !"
                (HISTORY OF GUSTAVUS VASA. JNO. MURRAY, *1852.*)

ness. While making his *Ericksgcit* through the kingdom, he often called the Evangelical clergy around
him and addressed them. He exhorted them to proceed cautiously in dealing with error and errorists, not
to dwell harshly on topics which might give offense,
not to carp at popes and bishops, for the ignorant people were immediately offended and said that they
preached a new faith. The pure doctrine of the Gospel he would certainly uphold and spread over the kingdom; but he complained that they did not instruct the
people properly; that some spoke scoffingly of the saints;
that some condemned good works, not distinguishing
those of man's device from those which God Himself
had ordained; that some had put aside holy days together with the comfortable Gospels and Epistles appointed for them; and finally that many led lazy and
scandalous lives. In these informal *conciones ad clerum*
the king had reference to the errors and misdoings of
both Papists and extreme and fanatical Protestants,
and showed himself a sound theologian as well as a
skillful administrator. But it cannot be denied that,
pressed on many sides with the conflicting demands
of his position, the necessity imposed upon him to be
at the same time a conservative and a reformer, led
him sometimes into dissimulations difficult to be reconciled with godly simplicity and sincerity.

The King's Treatment of the Priests and Monks. The king's strong conviction that the moral
and material welfare of the kingdom de-
pended upon taking from the clergy their
enormous privileges, and detaching their hold
upon the superstitious devotion of the people, through
a reformation of doctrine, led him to adopt a definite
and determined policy. In this determination he was
greatly encouraged and confirmed by his able Chan-

cellor, Lars Anderson. Anderson had been an ecclesiastic; but from a secret rejection of the Romish
system rather than from a cordial adoption of Lutheranism, he abandoned the clerical for the secular life;
and by his great knowledge and administrative ability
soon rose to the highest civil office in the kingdom,
and became the confidential counselor of the king. It
was from the standpoint of a statesman that he urged
the king to prepare the way for the establishment of
Lutheranism by depriving the clergy, first of many of
their prerogatives and immunities, and then of the
great possessions which these unjust advantages had
enabled them to accumulate. Very skillfully did he
begin to deprive them of those traditional or recognized rights which weighed most heavily upon the
people, in order that they might be won to approve
and sanction his proceedings. His measures in this
direction and to this end are thus described by Vertot
(p. 211): "The Swedish curates had assumed a right
to impose a kind of tax upon certain public sins, and
with a great deal of vigor exacted considerable fines
from those who took the diversion of hunting or fishing
in time of divine service, and those who abused women
to whom they were contracted before the solemn celebration of the sacrament of Marriage. This privilege
was abrogated by one of the king's proclamations, and
the priests were prohibited to exact such impositions
for the future. By another declaration they were forbidden to use ecclesiastical censures against their
private enemies or creditors. The bishops and their
officials had extended the jurisdiction of the Church
so far beyond its ordinary limits that they claimed a
divine right to take cognizance of all sorts of affairs
that had the least relation to religion. An oath made

in a bargain, the interposition of a clergyman which was frequently begged for that purpose, or the least dispute which arose about a contract of marriage were reckoned sufficient grounds to remove a cause from the ordinary courts of justice. But Gustavus abrogated their jurisdiction entirely, insinuating at the same time that the hearing and determination of suits were inconsistent with the function and duty of clergymen. And by the same declaration it was ordained that the clergy should be obliged to refer their differences to secular judges, who were authorized to take cognizance of all the affairs in the kingdom."

Further limitation of the Privileges of the Clergy. These were sweeping innovations. But Gustavus proceeded farther. He forbade bishops, on any pretense of right or of specific bequest, to take the property of deceased clergymen to the prejudice of their lawful heirs. As he saw that the Lutheranism which he secretly fostered progressed in the kingdom, he continued to issue injunctions which limited more and more the privileges of the bishops and the clergy.

Having thus prepared the way, the king was resolute in carrying out the policy which he had determined to adopt in reference to the ecclesiastical estates. It was estimated by him that the clergy were in possession of two thirds of the entire wealth of the kingdom; and he insisted that it was but just that they should bear a proportionate part of the burdens of the State, and not allow them to be borne only by the poorer classes, upon whom they had always pressed heavily, and in the present exigency would fall with crushing weight. As early as 1522 he had demanded aid from the clergy; and again in 1523 another requisition in the form of a loan was made; and in the three years succeeding the same demands continued to be enforced. When these continued exactions were followed by a dearth of food so severe as almost to amount to a famine in 1527 and 1528, the clergy did not fail to represent it as a visitation of God upon the kingdom for the oppression of the Church and the favor shown to the new heresy of Luther. These charges Gustavus met by the statement that it was but just that the clergy should contribute to the expenses of the State; that they were not taxed in larger proportion to their wealth than other classes; and that much of the property which he demanded of them was lying idle, and should be rendered available for the uses of the State. He declared that when he compelled them to bear their portion of the public burdens, and endeavored to protect the people from their exactions, they at once raised the clamor that all these measures were adopted with a view to introduce the Lutheran heresy and overthrow the Church. In replying to this charge, Gustavus insisted that in this proceeding he acted wholly in the character of a just ruler, and not as a Reformer. Without denying that he had protected Reformers, he declared that his protection of his subjects from unjust exactions and the arbitrary will of the priesthood should not be laid to the charge of innovating and reforming religious zeal.

His language upon the subject is very emphatic. He does not allow the bishops and priests to escape his specific charges by hiding them under the counter charge of Lutheran heresy and schism. "Certain monks and priests," he writes in 1526 to the people of Helsingfors, "have brought us into scandal, chiefly for that we blame their irregularities." Among these the king reckons that if a man owe anything, they refuse him the Sacrament, instead of pursuing their demand by law; if a poor man on a holy day kills a bird, or draws a fish from a stream, he is forthwith obliged to pay a fine to the bishop and the provost for Sabbath-breaking; that the laymen have not the same rights against the priests as the priests have against them; that the priests took the inheritance of priests dying intestate, passing over their heirs; that the clergy fraudulently possess themselves of much of crown property, and embezzle the king's proportion of judicial fines; when they perceive that we look to the interest of the crown, which is incumbent on us by reason of our kingly dignity, they straightway declare that we wish to bring in a new faith and Luther's doctrine; whereas the matter is not otherwise than ye have now heard, that we will not permit them to give loose to their avarice, contrary to law."

While it is evident that no devout Romanist could have used this language, and adopted these energetic measures, it is equally clear that they might have been employed by a just and decided king, who had no tendency to Lutheranism, nor even any religious convictions. They betray a rejection of Romanism, but not an adoption of Lutheranism.

Intrigues against the King. It was but a few months after his election that there were plots on foot to dethrone him, and to restore the house of Sturé to the head of the government. It seemed to be a circumstance favorable to the stability of his throne, that on his accession all the bishoprics, with the exception of two, were vacant. It might have fairly been expected that those whom he appointed would be loyal to him. But they all, sooner or later, became his enemies. Peter Jacobson, called Sunanvader, who had been chancellor of Steno Sturé the Younger, was

choson Bishop of Westeras by the Dalesmen, and
confirmed by the king.   But in less than a year he was
detected in a conspiracy to overthrow Gustavus, and
reinstate the house of Sturé.   He was deprived of his
office, as was also the newly elected Bishop Canute, who
appeared in his defense.   The deposed bishops proceeded to the Dales, and there fanned the conspiracy
which they had before kindled.   Their intrigues with
the Dalesmen led the latter to adopt a high tone
towards Gustavus, as if, being a king of their making,
they could direct him or depose him.   But it was not
long before they found that they had in him a master
who was just and generous to the loyal, but who could
be stern and terrible to the rebellious.   This they had
not learned as yet, and hence they assumed to address
him in the tone of those who felt that he would be
compelled to yield.   Under the dictation of the two
bishops they wrote to him that they would not permit
him to impose one tax after another upon the churches,
and convents, and priests, and monks, and people.
They renounced their allegiance to him unless he
procured for them cheaper markets, and drove foreigners from his service, and cleared himself from the
charge of having imprisoned Christina Gillenstierna,
and poisoned or banished her son.   They reminded
the king of his obligation to them "when he was a
friendless wanderer in the woods," and how ill he had
performed the promises which he made to them.

These intrigues were implicated with others which
rendered the position of the king for a time perilous
and doubtful.   So far from having imprisoned Christina,
Gustavus had just secured her release from a Danish
prison, when this charge was made.   She proceeded to
Calmar and there met her eldest son, Nicholas, who

was then twelve years of age, and whom the bishops
wished to elevate to the throne. It was at this time
that Norby, at the instigation of the bishops, attempted
to secure the hand of Christina, with a view to elevate
her son to the throne, of which they might be the joint
guardians. While Gustavus suspected Christina as secretly favoring this arrangement, he professed to regard
it as the mere gossip of the disaffected, and took the
young Sturé to his court for a time, and then sent him
to his mother, who had repaired to Upsala. His death
soon after removed the nucleus around which these intrigues and treasons gathered. For it was the double
object of many of these conspirators to elevate the house
of Sturé and restore King Christian. We learn that
this was the design of one party from a written promise
of the fugitive king, that if Lord Severin should marry
the Lady Christina, and thereby come into the government of Sweden, he might hold the kingdom absolutely
as the king's Lieutenant, for a yearly tribute. He even
issued a public letter to the effect that he had transferred his power to Norby until he should himself return
to his dominions. Norby in the spring of 1525 made a
descent upon Scania, and all the province except Malmö
again did homage to Christian. And at the same time
that this treason was working in the south of the kingdom, the rebel bishops were endeavoring to stir up the
dissatisfied Dalesmen to open opposition. But in this
they met with so little success,—the Dalesmen much
preferring to reprove Gustavus than to fight with him,
—that ultimately they were compelled to flee to Norby.
The Atti- It was under these complicated and harass-
tude of the ing difficulties that Gustavus exhibited at
King. once the enormous energy and resources of
his genius, and that stern side of his character which

sometimes passed into cruelty, which overawed at length all but the boldest and most desperate of his enemies. His firm attitude at the period, and his determination to put down the priesthood which so constantly employed its spiritual power to further temporal interests, appears in his spirited reply to the Dean of Upsala, who had pointed out to him what he regarded as the chief cause of popular discontent. " You write," replies the king, " that the people were angry that the Bishop of Westeras has not a sufficient number of retainers. We should rather expect them to be angry if they came with a multitude, burdening first one and then another; but *you* and many others, perhaps, may take offense thereat; you who cannot, or will not, think otherwise that that to the office of a bishop is attached some great worldly dignity, notwithstanding that the Scriptures hold them to be servants of all, and that they can fulfill this duty far better with few retainers than with many.

" You write further that it is highly desirable that nothing be violently or unjustly taken from the churches and monasteries. Would to God that our forefathers had been as careful that nothing had been filched from the crown and nobles by fraud and imposture, as folks nowadays take care to keep what they have obtained, whether by right or by wrong. We do not know whether we have taken anything violently from churches and monasteries as you write; but we know that we have restored them what their enemies had sliced away, and preserved what was threatened to be sliced away in like manner.

" Another person is now bestirring himself—I mean King Christian—making much ado to regain the Kingdom of Sweden—which God forbid! You will find, should he succeed, that he will filch more from you and from others than what we have either done or wish to do; and if you and the Chapter had well considered, you would have been quite as well advised had you defended our proceedings, instead of aggravating the case, whenever the priests who were under you had taken them ill or misunderstood them. If you yourself had given the matter due consideration, you, Master John, had no good grounds to fall in so readily with those who batter at our shield; and though you write that you do so with the best intentions, we can well perceive from your style to which side you incline. Now you are the man in whom of all in Upsala we have placed the most confidence—you are he whom we have highly exalted—you are he whom we have most delighted to know. See that you prove yourself sensible of this."

We cannot wonder that the treason of bishops of his own appointment, and the selfish greed and the thinly veiled disloyalty of friends in whom he trusted, should have awakened this feeling of scorn and indignation in the heart of the king; but it is only a brave man that, in the critical circumstances in which he was placed, would have ventured to give them such free expression. It is evident that he felt that the time had come for the inevitable conflict with the Papal and priestly power. He no longer disguised his conviction that the Church was not only an oppressive domination, fatal to the advancement and prosperity of the kingdom, the robber of the rights and possessions of citizens and of the State, in the name of religion, but that it was essentially anti-Christian in its dogmas and its spirit. He saw that the time for peaceful preparation for the Reformation had passed, and that it must either be established or destroyed by open conflict, by a decided victory or defeat. He did not hesitate to meet the crisis, not only with his usual magnificent intrepidity, but also with no little of passion and of polemic zeal. He put off his civic robes and threw down his diplomatic pen, and donned his armor and took in his mailed hand the sword that had won so many and such wondrous triumphs. The time was propitious. Christian was a fugitive. Frederic of Denmark was from policy friendly. Norby was out of the way. The Pope was in conflict with Charles V., and the Emperor's resources were too absorbed in that struggle, and in his large imperial schemes in Italy, the Netherlands and France, to allow him to intervene in the affairs of Sweden. His proceedings from this period plainly showed his purpose to grapple with and overthrow the Papal domination or to perish in the attempt.

CHAPTER IV.

THE resolution of the king to destroy the Papal power in Sweden soon found expression in measures which brought on an open conflict.

The Arrest and Execution of the two Bishops. Prompt steps were taken by the king to insure his authority over the people before he entered upon the decisive measure of securing the arrest and trial and punishment of the two rebel bishops. The States were assembled early in May, 1526, at Westeras. The king presented to them the two great evils which afflicted the country —the treason of the bishops, and the intrigues of Norby. He offered to resign his crown if his government was unsatisfactory to the States and people. But he was eagerly assured by them of their attachment to his person, of their loyal support to his government, and their co-operation in the punishment of traitors. Having thus received a fresh sanction to his authority, Gustavus proceeded to the Dales and summoned the people to meet him at Tuna-Kyrka, and held a conference with them, surrounding them by a considerable body of well-armed troops. Convinced by arguments and subdued by his commanding presence, and experiencing probably a renewal of their old affection and admiration, and perhaps overawed by the military display, which

was too large for a mere escort, and yet not so over-
whelming as to mortify them by the proof that they
were to be forced into submission, they acknowledged
that they had been misled, and promised not again to
be seduced from their allegiance.

Then he proceeded at once to secure the two rebel
bishops. They had fled to Norway and had found a
refuge with the Archbishop of Drontheim. The king
demanded them from the Norwegian Council by virtue
of an article of the treaty of Malmö, by which it was
agreed that the rebels of one country should not find
protection in the other. The Council consented to deliver up the refugees, but demanded a safe conduct for
them. Gustavus sent it in these terms: They should
experience no evil in coming to Sweden, but there they
should stand their trial before their proper judges, and
undergo what justice demanded and decreed. The
archbishop suggested that their proper judges were
prelates of the Church. But Gustavus would not listen
to this plea. He asserted justly that those who were
traitors to the State, should be tried by the civil power;
and not shelter their treason under a plea of religion.
It was evident that the safety of his throne depended
on the maintenance of this principle. He determined
to assert it in this case in a way so startling as to prove
to all that he was not to be deterred by any remaining
reverence for the Roman priesthood from punishing the
treason of ecclesiastics, with even more of rigor and
more accompaniments of disgrace, than those of civil-
ians. Sunanvader, who was ill, had been detained in
prison at Stockholm. When the archbishop was near
the city Sunanvader was carried out to meet him; and
a mock triumphal entry of the two took place. The
two bishops were seated, riding backwards, on half-

starved horses and in tattered Episcopal robes. On
the head of one was a miter of bark; the other wore a
crown of straw and a wooden half-broken sword. However much or little of significant symbolism might have
been intended by this travesty of power and office, it
was plain enough that there was in it an evident expression of defiance and contempt of the priesthood.
A few years earlier such an exhibition from whatever
cause would have created a revolt. But in this a great
crowd followed with demonstrations of approval, and a
group of masked men surrounded and followed them,
shouting, Here comes the new king, the Lord Peter
Sunanvader !

Sunanvader was sent to Upsala for trial. In addition
to the judges in the case of the archbishop, there were
added two bishops and the chief persons in the Chapter
of Upsala. The lay judges condemned the accused,
and the spiritual protested against their jurisdiction.
Petitions for mercy, strongly urged, were wholly un-
heeded by the king. The sentence was carried out at
Upsala upon the Bishop of Westeras in February, 1527,
and a few days after upon the archbishop at Stockholm.
Character of this proceeding. Gustavus has been severely censured, even
by Protestant historians, for this proceeding.
But it was evident that he could hold his
own, only by striking terror into the Papal party, and
by a distinct and sharp-cut issue, at this period, between the Reformation and the Papacy. It was no
more than justice towards the traitors, who used their
spiritual power for the overthrow of the government
as well as for the supremacy of the priesthood; and it
was as evidently good policy on the part of the king,
whose conscience was now enlisted in behalf of the
Reformation, and who both as a Christian and a patriot

was ready to stake his throne on the failure or success of his efforts to destroy the Papal and the priestly power.

The character of the policy of Gustavus from the first—the skillful use of conciliation where it was expedient, and of force and severity where it was necessary, is well described by Geijer in commenting on these proceedings. I quote part of the passage as affording a true key to the proceeding of the king during all his reign, in the midst of difficulties, which only a master mind could have overcome. He was a combination of Bismarck without his brutality, and of a Napoleon III. without his inertness.

" Men now began to be aware with whom they had to do; but they scarcely yet comprehended the full measure of that intrepidity which in Gustavus was usually evolved stroke by stroke as the resistance offered, and the circumstances of the case demanded, from a beginning that was tranquil and even apparently compliant. For such always was his commencement, unless urgent necessity prescribed a different line, and he ever went greater lengths than even his opponents expected. Signs like these announce to us a soul which teemed with a future yet unrevealed. Those who wish to study his character in this phase, from its earliest disclosure, may be referred to his correspondence with Bishop Brask, as one of the main sources of the history of the first year of his reign. This prelate was beyond camparison the most influential as well as the most sagacious and well-informed of his day in Sweden, and in his way an upright friend of his country. He treated the young king from the beginning with a kind of fatherly superiority, styling him 'dear Gustavus,' and accepting in return the title of 'gracious Lord.' Shortly after the election he obtained a

confirmation of all the privileges of his Church and bishopric. But he was soon forced to feel the significance
of the king's saying to the last Catholic archbishop,
Johannes Magnus: 'Thy grace and our grace have not
room beneath one roof.' With the aggressions of Gustavus on the clergy began the prelate's opposition; and
with every impediment thrown in his way the king
went one step further, as if he were more bent on re-
ducing his most powerful adversary to extremities, so
that the latter determined at length after the example
of Johannes Magnus to quit the kingdom. But he was
first to see the hierarchy of Sweden completely over-
thrown."

Deposition and Banishment of Johannes Magnus. A short time before these events Johannes
Magnus had incurred the king's displeasure,
both by his hostility to the Reformed doctrines, and his luxurious and extravagant
mode of life. He maintained a state and pomp which
surpassed that of the king's court. He made his Episcopal visitations with a cortege of two hundred persons;
and, like Cardinal Wolsey, he had among the pages
of his household the sons of some of the chief nobles
of the land. The king had in vain remonstrated with
him on his unseemly ostentation and luxury. On the
fair day of S. Eric he took the archbishop with him to
the old Upsala, and there on the summit of one of the
mounds, seated on horseback, with the people around
him, much to the disgust of the archbishop, he endeavored to convince them that there were too many
monks in the country, and that they were no better
than a race of vermin devouring the face of the earth;
and that it was an unreasonable thing to pray in Latin,
which they did not understand. The sturdy but superstitious peasantry called out that they would not

allow their monks to be driven out, but would themselves feed and sustain them.   This meeting took place
in May, 1526, and on their return to Upsala the king
accepted an invitation of the archbishop to a feast.
On that occasion the archbishop occupied a raised
seat on a level of that of the king, contrary to the usual custom on such occasions, and said while pledging
him "Our Grace drinks to your Grace."   The king answered, "For our Grace and your Grace there is not
room in the same house."   He rose from the table
much offended, and departed amid the smiles of the
courtiers, and the consternation of the ecclesiastics.
His dissatisfaction with the archbishop was much increased when at a conference with the Canons of Upsala he inquired of them on what they grounded their
right to their large possessions; and found that the
archbishop was determined to hold fast to the extent
of his ability to all the possessions and the old immunities of the Church.   Peter Gallé answered him that
these possessions were granted by nobles and others,
and confirmed by kings and princes.   "But," asked
Gustavus, "what if they have been obtained by fraud
—by preaching of purgatory or such-like cozenage of
priests and friars?"   The archbishop and the other
members of the Chapter, with the exception of George
Tureson, the dean, made no reply.   He boldly declared
that the gifts made by kings and emperors cannot be
filched away without God's curse and eternal damnation.

Upon suspicion of treasonable practices the archbishop was imprisoned for a time in a monastery; but,
without being tried, he was allowed to proceed to
Poland on the pretense of a mission to negotiate a
marriage between the king and the daughter of Sigismund.   But he furnished the archbishop with no

money; and it was evident that it was a device of the king to get him out of the kingdom. As soon as he was able to obtain means from his clergy, the archbishop proceeded at once to Dantzic, and thence to Rome, where he died in great poverty in the hospital of San Spirito, in 1537, and was buried in the Vatican.

Anti-Papal and Arbitrary Measures of the King. It was in the midst of increasing opposition and obstacles that the king himself took or sanctioned in others more and more decided measures against the devotions and practices and property of the Church. Olaus Petri took a wife in Stockholm in 1525. His example was soon followed by many other priests. Gustavus would not allow them to be deposed or to lose their position and emoluments. On the contrary, he wrote Bishop Brask that Olaus Petri would vindicate that proceeding by the Word of God. It was in this year also that the New Testament, translated at his request by the Chancellor, Lars Anderson, was published. In order to divert the interest and the ambition of the nobility away from the Church and towards the State, Gustavus conferred on them titles, and put them in possession of Church lands, which had been alienated from the estates of their ancestors, as he avowed, through the preaching of purgatory and other priestly cozenage.   .   *'*

We have seen that up to this period, 1525, Gustavus had insisted that the clergy should bear their proportionate part of the burdens of the State. But in that year, on account of the revolt of the Dalesmen and the attempts of Christian to recover the throne, and the diminution of the revenues, he went still further in his demand upon the revenues of the Church. At the meeting of the States in January, 1525, it was

agreed that the tithes, with the exception of so much
as should be necessary for wax-lights and the service
of the altar, should be appropriated to the pay of the
troops, and that the cavalry should be quartered upon
the monasteries. It was on this occasion that Bishop
Brask admonished the king not to appropriate tithes
to secular uses nor to encroach upon the privileges of
the convents. He declared "that as they were not
endowed from crown lands but by private property,
the king had not the smallest right to meddle with
them, neither had any previous monarch ventured to
do so." Gustavus answered in effect that he was compelled to this course by the necessity which knew no
law, and whether it were law or no, his course was
right in itself, and absolutely necessary in the emergency in which he was placed. After this, in 1526–27,
he took the ground distinctly that all Church property was the State's, and to be employed by it for the
best civil and religious welfare of the people. It was
inevitable that these sweeping claims, and the high-
handed enforcement of them which followed, would
lead to a decisive struggle of the old and new. To
enter fully into all the details of this struggle, in which
the interests of the Reformation were indeed involved,
but which were for the most part civil and military,
would be to lose sight for a time almost entirely of
the religious questions. This constitutes the special
difficulty of presenting the Reformation history—the
religious history of Sweden. It is to be discerned
through—lying under as it were—its civil history. In
some other countries the reverse of this is true, as in
Bohemia, and in England during the reigns of Henry
VIII., of Edward VI., and Elizabeth. There the civil
history is best seen under the religious history by

which it was shaped. But in Sweden, Gustavus was involved in his civil administration in difficulties arising from the exorbitant power of the clergy and the magnates and the turbulence of the people—difficulties which would have existed if no religious Reformation had been undertaken, but which were aggravated by this underlying, and, in the beginning, partially hidden purpose to dethrone the Papal power and introduce Lutheran Protestantism in its place.

Continued Appropriation of Church Property. After the decisive action of the States in Stockholm, in January, 1525, by which it was decreed that tithes should be appropriated to the payment of the troops, and the troops quartered upon the monasteries, the king more openly than before laid his hand upon the property of the Church. At a meeting of the States at Wadstena in the following year, on the same plea of State necessity, it was enacted that the beneficed clergy should bear the same burden in furnishing men at arms as the laymen of the same incomes. Gustavus also at this meeting confirmed the old privileges of the nobles and permitted them to redeem that portion of their patrimony which had passed into the hands of the Church since Charles Canutson's reign. It was a measure well calculated to enlist the lords on the side of the Reformation. Gustavus immediately availed himself of this provision to lay claim to the convent of Gripsholm. " You see," said Bishop Brask to his brother bishops on this occasion, " the fruit of your remissness. Our ruin is at hand, and you yourself have helped it on. The king, without a single remonstrance from you, has taken one step after another in overthrowing our religion. He has Lutheran priests in his palace preaching daily that our fall is near. He has attacked our monasteries and you have consented to his deeds. He has allowed priests to marry; he has in your very presence subjected our faith to examination. Now he snatches away our revenues, and you look on dismayed." "And," says one of the historians of Gustavus, "well might they do so! For against them was State necessity and a determined will and an almost absolute power; and they themselves were not so strong in truth and righteousness as not to blench before the formidable array."

The monks of Gripsholm hastened to lay the convent at the feet of Gustavus, not only without remonstrance but with abject expressions of satisfaction at the surrender. They close the document of transfer with these words: "If through misunderstanding of the affair any evil report should rise against his Grace in consequence of this proceeding, we pledge our honor and Christian faith that we will repel it and defend his Grace as we honestly may, well knowing that his Grace has good right to recover the inheritance which was taken by fort from his father."

Injustice of the King's proceedings against the Church of Abo. Thus far the king had secured the sanction of the States for his proceedings. But he seemed now to feel that he had become strong enough, through their support and sanction hitherto, to act without it, and of his own will to lay his hands on Church property, and arbitrarily to intervene in the management of Church affairs. He allowed dissatisfied monks on application to him to leave their monasteries. He wrote to the Bishop of Abo that the Chapter should have consulted him before they chose a dean, and prescribed to them as a sort of penance for their presumption that they should send 200 marks a year for the maintenance

of a good man—*i. e.*, one of his guard in the palace.
And what was more extraordinary, he ordered the
dean and chapter of the same See to change the late
dean's will. His missive on this occasion is certainly
a remarkable document, and is appended in order to
show the thoroughly arbitrary methods upon which
he had entered, and which led, not only to murmurs
and discontent, but ultimately to a new rebellion.

"We, Gustavus, hereby testify that it has been
made known to us how the good man, Jacob, Dean
of Abo, has left a large sum of money which he bequeathed in his will according to his pleasure; but it
is evident to any one who will duly consider the matter, that the said money could have been much better
disposed of; that is to say, that the greatest part of it
might have been applied to the public benefit, considering the burdens now lying on the country, through
the heavy debt occasioned by the war, which has been
now a long time waged against King Christian. We
therefore enjoin the Bishop and Chapter of Abo to
modify the said will according to our ideas, whic . we
have already partly explained to his executors, so that
while his heirs, relations and the poor get the share
that is given them, the rest may be applied, as far as
it will go, to the payment of the debt; when that
is done we acquit his executors of all other claim
from those interested in said will, whosoever they
may be."

It was impossible that such arbitrary proceedings should not excite murmurs and dissatisfaction.
Coupled as they were with the famine that followed,
and the increased heavy taxation, they led to a new
rebellion in Dalecarlia.

Rebellion in Dalecarlia. The prevailing disaffection, which ripened into revolt in Dalecarlia, gathered about a young impostor who professed to be the son of Sten Sturé. The youth whom he personated had been sent to Dantzic in 1520, and had returned to Calmar at the same time that Gustavus procured the liberation of Christina. He was at the time that this pretender appeared, 1527, at the court of Gustavus, who was falsely accused of having taken his life. It was this false rumor, propagated by the partisans of Christian and Norby, which gave rise to this attempt. The pretender declared that Gustavus had ordered that he should be killed, but that he escaped from the court of the heretic tyrant who had sought his life. A soldier of the late Regent, Peter Grym, assisted him in his deception and taught him how to play his part. He was an illegitimate child of an unknown father, and had acquired in the service of a nobleman the arts and manners which gave plausibility among the simple Dalesmen to his claim. He is described as handsome, eloquent, and full of assurance and assumption. Whenever he spoke of his pretended father it was with so much seeming feeling that the Dalesmen could not refrain from weeping with him. He thanked them for their love to his father, and bade them to pray for his soul. He proceeded to Norway, where he was taken up by the archbishop, and through his influence betrothed to a lady of large fortune and high family. Returning to the Dales with the aid he derived from Norway, he rallied some supporters, although opinion with regard to him was much divided, and he determined to resist the forces of the king. Christina Gyllenstierna, at the king's request, wrote to the Dalesmen disowning her pretended son.

Complaints of the Dales- men   After some skirmishing with the king's troops, the Dalesmen came to a parley with the com- missioners whom the king had sent to confer with them in reference to their alleged grievances. The complaints transmitted by the commission were answered by Gustavus with the patience which he could always display upon occasion, and which the critical circumstances in which he was now placed made expe- dient. They complained that there was but little coin in circulation, of heavy taxes, of dearness of provisions, and of the profanation of monasteries. One of the most curious of their grievances, and one which shows the simplicity of the times, and the freedom with which they addressed their kings, was their objection to the new-fashioned slashed doublets that were worn at court. They objected to the Lutheranism which prevailed at Stockholm, and the psalms and hymns that were sung in public worship. These and similar grievances, in which the gravest and most trivial matters were ab- surdly mixed, were answered fully and in their order by the king. New coin should soon be struck. The heavy taxes were unavoidable after the war, but would be di- minished as soon as peace was assured and Christian disabled from doing further mischief. The dearness of provisions was due to famine, which was God's visitation and should be borne with pious patience. He quite agreed with them about slashed doublets—he did not like them—but what could he do with giddy young courtiers who would adopt every foreign folly that was imported? And what concern was it of theirs how he and the courtiers dressed ? As to Lutheranism and the Swedish hymns, he answered—not very ingenuously— that he knew little about Lutheranism; but that he was determined to put a stop to priestly impositions and

secure the pure preaching of the Word of God; and that
it was certainly more sensible to sing hymns in Swedish
which they understood than in Latin of which they
were wholly ignorant. He expressed surprise that they
should meddle with questions such as these, which were
quite beyond their capacity, and not leave them to be
settled by the State Council and learned clerks and
prelates.

The result of these conferences and communications
of the king was that the Dalesmen agreed to lay down
their arms and abandon the pretender; and on the part
of Gustavus there was an assurance of complete oblivion
of all that had been done or attempted in his favor. It
was furthermore decided that a meeting of the States
should take place at Westeras in which all the questions
at issue between the king, the Dalesmen, and the clergy,
should be discussed and settled.

Meeting of the States in Westeras. This meeting of the States in Westeras, as
it was most important in view of the crisis
at which it was summoned and most mem-
orable for its results, was also remarkable for the unusual numbers for that age by which it was attended.
There were present, 4 Bishops, 4 Deans, 15 State Councillors, 120 Nobles, 32 Burghers (exclusive of the Town
Council of Stockholm, who were present and had a considerable influence upon their proceedings), 14 Miners,
representative of that important interest, and 105 peasants from all parts of the kingdom, except the Dales,
who felt that the question between them and the king
was one of the most important which was to be settled.
The nobles at the king's request came armed. He
reckoned on their support in striking the decisive blow
against the bishops and the clergy, upon which he was
resolved.

Gustavus opened the session on the Sunday before the midsummer's day by a magnificent banquet in which he conspicuously displayed his purpose to bring down the hierarchy. The indignities offered to Knut and Sunanvader might seem to have been prompted solely by their repeated treasons; the insults heaped upon Johannes Magnus to have been the due reward of his vanity and folly; but the king now determined to take a step which could not be mistaken. The whole hierarchy was now to be humbled. They had always been assigned the highest places in all public proceedings, and especially in feasts—the bishops taking position above even the regents of the kingdom. But on this occasion the place assigned them was below the State Council and the higher nobles.

This was no light matter in itself, and it was alarmingly significant as an indication of the intended policy of the king towards the prelates and the Church. The bishops met, with closed doors, in the church of S. Egedius, to consider the situation. Their leader, Bishop Brask, declared that the purpose of the king was patent. He no doubt intended to take away their revenues and castles and prelatical prerogatives, and degrade them to the level of mere parish priests. But to this, if they were wise, they never would consent. They could not indeed resist force; but they could wield a force greater far than that of kings'—even that of interdict and excommunication. Mightier monarchs than Gustavus had been prostrated by the thunders of the Church. Let them remain true to the Pope and their order and they might retain or recover their position; but if they yielded they would be held no better than serfs or cowards.

At Brask's suggestion the assembled dignitaries

signed a paper, in which they pledged themselves to protect the Church's rights, to be true to the Pope, never to adopt the Lutheran heresy, and to await with patience the change of government. They hid this document under the floor of the church, where fifteen years after it was discovered.

The King's Address. The king, through his chancellor, thanked the Diet for having assembled at his call, in the present emergency, in such large numbers. He reminded them that at Wadstena he had offered to resign the regency. In consequence of the state of the kingdom at that time he had been obliged to seek aid in Lubeck and other towns, and hence the large indebtedness and heavy taxes of the kingdom. After the surrender of Stockholm the nobles had chosen him king, and his election had been confirmed by all the orders of the State. He had then reluctantly accepted the office, and had since often repented having done so. "For," and here he dropped his apologetic and explanatory style, "who could rule with any comfort such a people? Who especially would desire to rule the Dalesmen, who were ever on the look-out for something to find fault with, ever ready to break into open revolt, if the king did not submit to their capricious and unreasonable demands? They were ever boasting that they had placed him upon the throne. But after the victory at Westeras, when the liberation was by no means fully assured, most of them went home again." Passing from this outburst of rebuke, the chancellor proceeded to vindicate the proceedings of Gustavus, in reference to the monasteries, the taxing of the clergy, the limitation of the powers of the bishops, and the introduction of the pure preaching of the Gospel. The king, he said, was more than ready to resign the throne if the people were dissatisfied and wished him to do so; but as long as he occupied it he was fixed in his purpose of pursuing the policy which under a deep sense of duty to his country he had hitherto adopted.

It was a bold but probably a politic proceeding on the part of the king. It was one of those decisive occasions on which a great man, driven at bay, and losing his temper and self-control, and regardless of consequences, assumes a defiant attitude which ultimately stands him in better stead than his usual more restrained and politic methods of proceeding. It was evident that he now stood at the turning point of his career, where he was either to be unseated or to be more firmly fixed in his position upon the throne. It was also clear that he had become so harassed that he had lost his usual patience and forbearance, and was really indifferent to the result. He did not desire to be king unless he could have the ample power necessary to discharge the office at an era so disturbed and among a people so independent in spirit, so prone to complain and to adopt a tone of dictation to their rulers. If he had attempted to wheedle or conciliate them we can scarcely doubt that he would have failed. By taking a high tone of indignation, which, unlike some of the first Napoleon's outbursts of feigned passion for evil ends, was genuine, and by the expression of more than willingness to resign his office, which was evidently real, the admiration of some of his opponents might be awakened, and others become alarmed at the view of the anarchy which would probably result from his abdication. Whether or no this result was in his thought, it was immediately brought about by the strong reaction which ensued.

Opposition to the King. The ruling spirit of the opposition, Bishop Brask, who could no longer doubt that the existence of the Romish Church in Sweden and the prerogatives of his own order depended on the result of this Diet—had arranged the method of proceeding, which he hoped would lead to the persistent refusal of Gustavus to wear a crown so lined with irritating cares, and the acceptance of his resignation by the States. He had induced Thuré Johnson, the senior member of the king's council, and therefore next to the king in position in the kingdom, to approve his views and second his efforts. Accordingly, when the address had been read and the king demanded an answer of the nobles and bishops, Thuré Johnson requested that Bishop Brask might give his opinion. Gustavus could not but have perceived that this proceeding had been pre-arranged, and this knowledge was by no means calculated to calm his excitement. The bishop replied to the appeal that he was well aware of the allegiance which he owed to the king; but he and all his order were equally bound to obey the Pope in things spiritual, and that without his concurrence he could not consent to any change of doctrine, nor to any diminution of the Church's rights and possessions. If, indeed, unscrupulous priests had sought to enrich themselves by working upon the superstitions of the laity—a course which the heads of the Church themselves condemned—let such cases be proved and punished.

The King's indignant speech, and resignation of the throne. The king asked the nobles and the State Councillors if this reply seemed to them sufficient. Thuré Johnson said that he could not but think that the Bishop's answer was in the main right, though not a complete reply to all that the king had brought forward. Gustavus was too indignant to measure his words, or even to re-strain himself within the bounds of his royal dignity. " Then," said he, " we have no will longer to be your king. From you we had expected another answer; but now we cannot wonder that the common people should give us all manner of disobedience and misliking, when they have such ringleaders. Get they not rain, the fault is ours; if sunshine fail them, it is the same cry; if bad years, hunger, and pest come, so must we bear the blame. All ye will be our masters. Monks and priests and creatures of the Pope ye set over our heads; and for all our toil for your welfare we have no other reward to expect than that ye would gladly see the axe at our neck; and there are none of you but gladly grasp its handle. Who would be your king on such terms ? Not the worst fiend in hell, much less a man ! Therefore look ye to it that ye release me fairly of the government, and restore to me that which I have disbursed of my own stock for the general weal. Then will I depart and never see again my ungrateful fatherland." The king, at these words, burst into tears, and hastily quitted the hall.

It is not often that such momentous results have hung upon one short speech. The Reformation in Sweden, the heroic services of Gustavus Adolphus in behalf of periled Protestantism in Europe, the prevention, it is not too much to say, of the crushing out of Protestant-ism in Germany—all these great issues hung suspended on the result of that short, impassioned speech.

The Conster-nation of the Diet. When Gustavus disappeared a deep silence fell upon the assembly. At length the chan-cellor came forward, and invited them in the great difficulty in which they were involved to offer up their united prayers to God for guidance. "We have only the alternative to choose, either to follow the king, as he has proposed, and entreat him to carry on the government, or to pay him what he has expended for the State, and to choose another king." They were, however, too much confounded by the scene which they had witnessed to determine anything that day. Thuré Johnson put on an appearance of resolution and bluster, and marched to his lodgings preceded by a drum, as if to announce a victory, and to express his joy at the result. He exclaimed, as he marched on, that "he defied any man to make him a Lutheran or a heathen." But when in the meeting on the next day the lords and clergy did not come to any decision, the peasants grew impatient, and said if all things were well considered Gustavus had done them no injury, and that unless the nobles soon settled something, they would take the matter into their own hands. The merchants and shop-keepers supported the peasants, and the burghers of Stockholm declared that they would hold that city for the king. Magnus Sommer, Bishop of Strengness, declared that the bishops did not wish to be so protected as to leave the kingdom a prey to its worst enemies. The declaration was received with great applause. Many declared that they would have no other king but Gustavus. They desired to hear a discussion upon the differences of the Catholic and the Protestant doctrines. Accordingly, Olaus Petri and Peter Gallé argued the question until late in the day. The peasants compelled Gallé, who commenced the discussion in Latin, to speak in Swedish. The impression left by this discussion was favorable to the Reformation.

The King induced to withdraw his Resignation. While these events were in progress in the Diet, Gustavus held his court at the castle surrounded by his military staff, and passed the time with them in various diversions. His whole bearing was that of a man who had been relieved of a heavy burden. But on the third day the burghers and the peasants said to the nobles that if they chose to be the ruin of the king and kingdom, they with the aid of the king would ruin them; and that they had already sent a message to the king to that effect. Thereupon several of the nobles entreated Thuré Johnson to cease his opposition to the king. He sullenly agreed to do so, on condition that the king would agree not to lead the people into any heresy. The Diet accepted his consent, and took no notice of the condition which he attached to it.

Thereupon Lars Anderson and Olaus Petri were sent to Gustavus to entreat him still to hold the throne. They were met with a short and sharp refusal. On their return they prayed that if any further communications were to be made to the king, it might be by other messengers. Knut Anderson and the Bishop of Strengness undertook the task; but they also came back unsuccessful. The anxiety now became intense. The future before the Diet now seemed to be a civil war, and the re-appearance and perhaps the reinstatement of King Christian. The prospect was too dreadful to be contemplated with composure. All opposition vanished, and the Diet became an importunate supplicant. The last committee that was sent to the king fell on their knees and wept. The king at length relented, and consented to meet the States on the following day. His long resistance to these appeals can as well be reconciled—perhaps better—with the theory that he was

sincere in his purpose to abdicate the throne, as to that
which would regard the whole proceeding as a skillful
scheme to bring the Diet to his feet, and to secure their
pledges of unconditional surrender and obedience. For
if he were sincere and desirous to withdraw from a conviction that he could not succeed in his government,
unless the lords and people became more loyal to him,
and more ready to aid him in putting down the priestly
party, he certainly would refuse to revoke that decision,
and persist in his refusal until he should be convinced
that such a change had been wrought in the feelings
of his opponents as would seem to furnish a guaranty
that hereafter he might rely upon their hearty co-
operation and support.

On his appearance in the Diet, attended by his State
Council and a splendid life-guard, he was received with
hearty demonstrations of applause. Now the three estates, the nobles, burghers, and peasants, with one voice
sanctioned his demands.

Gustavus had triumphed. His foes were, for the time
at least, silenced, if not reconciled. Thus far the Reformation has been seen struggling for life and recognition. Hereafter we shall see it established, indeed, but
violently opposed, and still compelled to unceasing
warfare with foes who postponed its complete ascendency, and hindered its full development. During all the
remainder of the reign of Gustavus, his· history at the
same time *is* or *involves* the history of the Reformation.

CHAPTER V.

FROM the Diet of Westeras may be dated the establishment of the Reformation in Sweden. But
its progress during the reign of Gustavus was slow, and
in that of Eric it was arrested and temporarily paralyzed.
Decrees of the Diet of Westeras. The demands or propositions of the king,
according to the custom of the Swedish
Diets, were not voted upon by a body as
a whole, but were answered by each class for itself.
Accordingly there was not the same cordial acquiescence in all the answers that were rendered; and the king
could judge by the tone of the reply how far he could
rely upon the loyalty and support of the class by which
it was given. The bishops gave a forced submission
to the decrees, but after this period they were no longer
summoned to the Diet. The decree of the Diet contained, 1. A mutual engagement to resist all attempts
at rebellion. 2. A grant of power to the king to take
in his own hands the castles and strongholds of the
Bishops; to fix their revenues and those of the canons
and prebends; to levy fines and to regulate monasteries.
3. Authority was given to the nobles to resume the
lands which had been conveyed to churches and
monasteries since the inquest of Charles Canutson, if

they could substantiate their claims before a court, and by a verdict of a jury. 4. Liberty was assured to the preachers "to proclaim the pure Word of God," "but not," the barons added, "uncertain miracles, human inventions and fables."

We can see in the answer of the burghers and peasants concerning the faith their lingering misgiving and indisposition to give to it an emphatic assent. They declare that inquiry should be made into it, but that the matter passed their understanding. The bishops declared "that they were content, however rich or poor his grace would have them to be." In the supplement of the statute called "The Ordinance of Westeras" the bishops are authorized to fill up the vacant benefices, but if they should appoint murderers, drunkards, or such as should be unable to preach God's Word, that they might be displaced and others of the king's appointment substituted. It was provided that fines for fornication should be paid to the king and not to the bishops. No fines shall be inflicted for working on saints' days. The bishops were to render to the king an account of the revenues, that he might settle what portion they would be permitted to retain. The clergy should be amenable, in secular affairs, to the civil jurisdiction. The property of the deceased clergy should fall to their lawful heirs, and not to the bishops. Mendicant friars should be permitted to leave their convents to beg only for five weeks in the summer, and five in the winter. The sick should not be forced by the priests to make a will. The clergy should not withhold the Sacrament at Easter, or any other time, for the debts due to themselves. And, finally, the Gospel should be taught to the children in all the schools.

It is clear that if Gustavus had not just won a victory

over his foes, and been tacitly admitted, even by them, as necessary to preserve the State from anarchy and intestine war, he could not have acquired such mastery over the Diet as that which induced them or forced them to pass this sweeping and radical decree. The particulars enumerated in the decree exhibit at once the degraded condition of the clergy, the enormous power and possessions of the bishops, and their rapacious robbery of the rights and possessions of the people. They lived in fortified castles as feudal lords. They rode forth from them on episcopal progresses and visitations, attended by hundreds of military body-guards. Under the control of the Bishop of Linkoping there were more than six hundred benefices and estates; under the Bishop of Abo more than four hundred, and under the Archbishop almost as many as both of them combined. Never was a poor and small kingdom so oppressed and impoverished by a grasping and lordly hierarchy. That, while the great body of the people had not yet accepted the reformed faith, nor emancipated their minds from absolute and abject submission to the clergy, Gustavus should have been able to pass and enforce these decrees, without exciting a revolution, demonstrates the imperial ascendency of his character, by the blended skill and courage with which he overcame the manifold difficulties of his position.

The King's Treatment of the Bishops. When all these provisions had been confirmed, the king immediately turned to the bishops and demanded first from the Bishop of Strengness the Castle of Tilnelsö, which the latter declared himself ready to surrender. The same answer was returned by the Bishop of Skara to the demand of the Castle of Leckö. But when the king came to Bishop Brask and demanded his castle,

"silence and sighs," says Geijer, "were the only reply."
Thuré Johnson begged for his old friend that the castle
might be spared him during h··· lifetime, but the king
answered shortly, "No." Eight lords of the council
were obliged on the spot to become sureties for the
bishop's obedience. Forty men of his body-guard were
taken from him, and enrolled in the king's army. At the
same time the king sent commissioners to the principal
churches and monasteries of Sweden to take account
of their endowments, revenues and possessions. Bishop
Brask succeeded, by a seeming submission, in freeing
himself from the securities which he was obliged to
give; and on the pretense of going on a sort of missionary expedition to the island of Gothland, he escaped
to Poland, and made his way to Rome, where he died.
He was the most eminent man, next to Gustavus, of
that generation in Sweden; and it is by no means
certain that the king did not know and rejoice in his
intended expatriation. Whether the indignation which
he expressed at the bishop's escape was feigned or
real, it gave him an opportunity to say to him some
things which were all the more cutting because they
were true. He wrote to him "that formerly good
men were reluctant to take the Episcopal office, but
when once they had entered on it they would willingly
die for it, and would not be separated from their sheep
until driven from them. It is not so with you, but you
have done quite the contrary. You pressed into the
office, and without necessity or compulsion have fled from
it. As long as the case was such that you could milk,
shear and slay the flock, you were right at hand; but
when the Word of God came and said that you should
feed the flock of Christ, and not shear and slay them,
then you fled." (Anjou: Reform in Sweden, p. 242.)

Fall of the Monastic System. There was an article in the Ordinance of Westeras which provided for the mainte-nance of the *existing* members of the relig-ious houses "that they might praise and serve God." In the mood of mind of Gustavus towards all the pa-pal clergy, and especially towards the monks, it was scarcely to be expected that this provision should be very strictly observed. The States assembled at Up-sala in 1528 complained of the king that, instead of observing that article, he had induced monks and nuns to leave their convents and to marry, and had expelled others whose conduct was reprehensible, instead of leaving them to the chastisement of their ecclesiastical superiors. No doubt pressure was brought to bear upon the monasteries by Gustavus to induce them to make an early surrender. When the whole matter in general terms was put in the hands of the king, it is not surprising, in view of the gross vices that prevailed in many of these institutions, that a man of so decided character as Gustavus should not allow himself to be arrested in his work by technicalities. He was em-powered to break them up; the sooner they were de-stroyed the better would the interests of morality and the welfare of the kingdom be subserved. This was the summary logic which satisfied his mind. No doubt the great good that was accomplished was accompanied with instances of individual suffering; but if reformations waited until no one could suffer from them, they would never come.

The Episco-pal Succes-sion. It is to be observed that adherence to the Papal Church was not, as in England, for-bidden and punished with fines and penal-ties. The bishops were not dispossessed of their sees. They were deprived, indeed, of a large part of their

emoluments, and exhorted to preach the pure Word
of God, and were not permitted to punish heretics
or to brand Protestantism as heresy; and they were
stripped of many of their old prerogatives and privileges. There was no fanatical war, as in Scotland,
against the Episcopal order as such, but only against
its overgrown immunities and privileges and its enormous power. On the contrary, it was the effort of
the Government to bring over the bishops to the acceptance of the new faith by influence, and by com-
pensations for the losses to which they were subjected.
They were not at once to be deprived, but to hold
their sees with diminished revenues and with increased
amenability to the Government and the civil law; but
in the mean time they were exhorted and encouraged
to come into harmony with the new system, and to
carry it out in their dioceses; and by this means it
was hoped that some of them would from conviction
adopt the system upon which the Reformation was
founded. The policy was not unlike that by which
James II. sought to bring back the bishops of the
Church of England to the Church of Rome.

The question of the Episcopal succession, to which
so much importance has been attached in modern
controversy, seems to have been scarcely mooted.
The native historians do not allude to it as a vital
question. The old sees, with vastly diminished revenues and privileges, were retained, and it seems to have
been by a natural and unforced train of circumstances,
rather than by a careful design and arrangement, that
the Episcopal succession was preserved. It is evident
from the subsequent proceedings of Gustavus, as we
shall see, that he attached no special importance to
the preservation of the unbroken Episcopal succession,

and that he would have been satisfied that the Episcopal sees, as in Denmark, should have been filled by
those who had only the ordination of presbyters; and
who, while they bore the name of bishops, should in
fact have no higher functions and jurisdiction than the
superintendents of the Lutheran Church in Germany.
It is only in a brief foot-note that the great national
historian, Geijer, mentions the method in which the succession was secured. In enumerating the four bishops
that were in the Diet of Westeras, he names them thus:
"There were present four Bishops, viz.: Brask, of Linkoping; Magnus Harolson, of Skara; Magnus Sommer,
of Strengness, and Peter Magnusen, of Westeras,—the
latter being the only one besides Brask who had received his consecration, which was performed at Rome.
At the king's special request, after Peter Sunanvader
had been deposed, *this Peter Magnusen afterwards
consecrated the bishops appointed by the king*." It was
by the consecration of this single bishop that the succession has been preserved in Sweden.

If, therefore, one deems the unbroken Episcopal succession necessary to the existence of a valid ministry,
and to the intercommunion of the Episcopal Church
with other churches, he will undoubtedly find that it
has been preserved in the Church of Sweden. This has
been conclusively proved by Dr. A. Nicholson, of Leam-
ington, for several years English Consular Chaplain at
Gothenburg. He recently returned to Sweden, and in-
vestigated the question anew, and has produced proofs
which are indisputable, that the succession has been
preserved in the Church of Sweden. He concludes his
documentary and complete evidence in these words:
"Those who doubt the Apostolic succession of the
bishops of the Church of Sweden ignore facts, and con-

found that Church with the Danish and Norwegian bodies. Hence arise their prejudices upon the subject, which are not more reasonable than the Roman suspicion that Barlow and Parker were English laymen, and are not less fanciful, let me add, than the corresponding prejudice existing to-day in the mind of the Swedish High Churchman against the English, as one of those sects which owe their rise to the accidents of the Reformation, and their doctrines on the Holy Sacraments and on Grace to Zwinglius and Calvin" (p. 57). Thus Dr. Nicholson, while graciously admitting that the Swedish Church possesses the succession, and may therefore be acknowledged by the Anglican Church, receives in return from Swedish Churchmen the contemptuous statement that his own Church is a mere sect, the creature of an accident, and unsound in the faith on fundamental points!

Coronation of Gustavus and the Execution of the Pretender. The coronation of Gustavus took place at Upsala, in February, 1529. It was observed on that occasion that contrary to the usual custom no one bore the crown. It stood upon the high altar, and Gustavus was believed to intimate thereby that he received it direct from heaven. As the Dalesmen continued refractory, and kept up correspondence with the pretended Sturé in Norway, Gustavus marched an army of 14,000 men into the Dale district, and assembled a large number of the people at what was called the Assize of Tuna, and demanded that the chief supporters of the Daleyunker, as the Pretender was called, and especially those who constituted his council, should be surrendered to him. Resistance was impossible, and a large number of those most active in the support of the Yunker were, after a short trial, executed. The surrender of the false Sturé was demanded from the Archbishop of Drontheim, but evaded by sending him disguised to Rostock; but he was discovered in that city by the agents of the king, and tried and executed for treason. It was a severe proceeding, but probably not more so than the emergency demanded.

Lutheran- ism in the Ascendant. The time was now ripe for an open acknowledgment and support of the Protestant faith by the king. The most powerful supporters of the old system had abandoned the field. Most of the clergy avowed their acquiescence in the Protestant faith, and retained their parishes. The king declared himself a Lutheran. He appointed Olaus Petri Pastor of the Church at Stockholm, and his brother Laurentius Petri was subsequently, 1531, elected Archbishop of Upsala. The flight of Bishop Magnus and Bishop Brask greatly forwarded the progress of the Reformation. The consecration of three new Bishops by Bishop Magnus enabled him to be consecrated by them without taking the old form of the oath to protect the holy Church. At that coronation it was observed also, as a significant sign, that he did not, according to the old formula, receive the crown from the hand of the archbishop, but left it lying upon the altar, in token of his acceptance of it directly from God. And the sermon of Olaus Petri on that occasion was plainly and emphatically Protestant. From that time the indefatigable Olaus Petri, the polemic and the doctrinal leader of the Reformation, published within a year no less than nine treatises on the points at issue between Lutheranism and Romanism. They covered the whole ground of the reformed theology. In this work he was powerfully aided by Lars Anderson, Archdeacon of Upsala, whose shaping and systematizing mind brought the new doctrines into a coherent order. They were the Luther and Melancthon of the Swedish Reformation, and the coming Diet of Orebo was their Diet of Augsburg, and its Decrees their Confession.

Moderation of the Reformers. But although the king and his two principal spiritual aids and advisers were thoroughly Protestant Reformers, they were not iconoclasts and radicals. While they established a doctrinal reform and rejected the false and deadly dogmas of the Papacy, and swept away with a strong hand the practical corruptions and superstitions of the Church of Rome, they prudently allowed some points of ritual and ceremonial to remain, especially in the cathedral churches, in order that there might be less shocks to the minds of the weaker Reformers, and of the common people. We find, for instance, that in the cathedral of Linkoping " six prelates and canons should remain in the cathedral with the best prebends, and keep ten priests to bear crosses, the bishop two, the provost two, the archdeacons two, the four canons each one. In the cathedral of Wexio arrangements were made that there should be four canons with the best prebends and six cross-bearing priests and a school." (Anjou, p. 230.) These were specimens of what was still allowed to remain of the great staff of ecclesiastics and officials that had before thronged the cathedrals. Moreover the principal festivals commemorative of the life and death of the Saviour were retained, and rich vestments were worn in the administration of the Lord's Supper, and the cross was still borne in processionals, and in some cases the crucifix was not removed from the Holy Table.*

* It is a curious anomaly in a church which exalts so highly the doctrine of the Lord's Supper, and clothes its priests in gorgeous garments in its admin-

It is another notable evidence of the moderation of the Swedish Reformation that it not only did not proscribe and disfranchise the Roman Church, and subject its priests as such to penalties and punishments, but that it endeavored to bring over the bishops and priests to an acceptance of the new faith by a system of instruction and influence and rewards. The bishops were not at once to be dispossessed, but to hold their sees with diminished revenues and privileges, and with increased amenability to the government and civil law; but in the meantime they were exhorted to come into harmony with the new system and to work it out in their dioceses; and by this means it was hoped that some of them would ultimately from conviction adopt the principles upon which the Reformation was founded. The policy was not unlike that by which James II. sought to bring back the prelates of the Church of England to the Church of Rome. The policy of Gustavus succeeded partially among the lower clergy, but failed almost wholly to bring over the dignitaries of the Church.

Although the monasteries became the property of the crown, and the king immediately dissolved most of them, yet even here there was the same moderation displayed as in the matter of ritual and ceremonial. They were not all at once swept out of existence, in

istration, that it leaves its chancels or sanctuaries unadorned, and in some cases in a condition of shameful untidiness and neglect. The author observed this to be the case in all the churches—not many it is true—which he saw in a recent tour through Sweden. He was amazed to find that the great Cathedral of Upsala, the Metropolitan Cathedral, and the greatest in the kingdom, contained a very small chancel, constructed of plain pine wood, much worn, with appointments which were absolutely shabby, and the whole wearing an aspect of great neglect. I venture to say that there is not in all the churches which I have seen in the city of Philadelphia, one chancel that is not superior in its appointments, and more reverently cared for, than that of the grand Cathedral of Upsala.

cruel disregard of helpless and blameless inmates. Some few cloisters remained after the death of Gustavus. That of Sko was standing in 1556, and those of Wadstena and Nadendal in 1595. Many of them were converted into hospitals and some into schools for the education of youths.

The Synod of Orebo. The Synod of Orebo was opened on the 2d of February, 1529. As the Archiepiscopal See of Upsala was not yet filled, it was represented by Lars Anderson, who was appointed President. The assembly was thus constituted as a National Synod. Besides the three bishops—neither of whom was cordially in favor of the Reformation—there were nineteen canons, eleven rectors of the larger churches, eight monks and many of the parochial clergy. No record of the preceedings and debates of the council, with the exception of the decree which it passed, remains. If its members were not overawed by the knowledge that the eye of the king was on them, the debates in an assembly so composed must have been earnest, if not stormy. But, whatever might have been the secret opinions of some of its members, the decree included but little that was not distinctly Protestant. It may be divided into three heads, (1) preaching, (2) discipline, (3) church usages and ceremonies. The principal provisions, were these: Better provision shall be made for the preaching of the Gospel over the realm. The bishops were enjoined to preach, and to secure well instructed preachers, under the penalty of losing their benefices. One lesson at least from the Scriptures, with a good and sound exposition was ordered to be read daily in the cathedrals and public schools. The lectures of the schools should be so arranged that the choristers should have an opportunity of attending them. Learned preachers

were to be appointed in towns, to whom all rural preachers
might resort for instruction. Afternoon lectures were
to be delivered in the monasteries. Sermons were to
be begun and ended with prayer. At every preaching,
the Creed, the Lord's Prayer and the Ave Maria (which
it was not thought prudent yet to set aside) were to be
repeated; the ten commandments also were to be read
twice a month.

In the matter of discipline the Penitentiaries were
strictly enjoined to use more sharpness with manslay-
ers and other criminals. As the frequent Holy Days
gave much occasion to rioting and sin, it was ordered
that our Lord's own festivals, the Virgin's, the Apos-
tles' and those of the national patron saints should be
retained, and the rest abolished. Scholars were forbidden to go from parish to parish to collect alms, as
the custom gave rise to many abuses. Marriage of the
priests was allowed. The Penitentiaries of the cathedrals were empowered to use such severity in their
dealings with murderers as they should see fit, and
this exceptional power to inflict civil penalties for
crimes was placed on the singular ground that "the
worldly sword appears to be idle, and has not the
force that it ought to have." Each bishop may limit
the number of saints' days as he shall judge to be
most for edification.

In the explanation of church ceremonies, there is
an effort made to show their true and salutary use and
meaning as distinguished from the superstitions which
had gathered about them in the public mind. Consecrated water cannot take away sin, for that is effected only
by the blood of Christ. Images are not for worship, but
only for bringing Christ and the saints into remem-
brance. Candlemas lights have no enlightening power

for the mind, but are only symbols of the true light of
the world, Christ Jesus. Chrism does not convey, but
is only a sign of the Holy Ghost. The ringing of bells
has no power over evil spirits, but is of use only in
calling the people to Church. "Church structures are
kept up, not for any peculiar sanctity in themselves,
for the worship of God, but that men may meet together there and learn God's Word." "Fast days are
kept, not as special worship done to God, but to tame
our lustful bodies." Explanations similar to these concerning saints' days and pilgrimages follow. Such was
the system on which the Reformation was established
in Sweden, and such substantially it continued under
manifold difficulties, which hindered its complete ascendency, during the whole reign of King Gustavus.

Insurrec- It was inevitable that such great changes,
tions and however skillfully prepared for and gradu-
Commotions. ally introduced, would awaken opposition
and lead to popular commotions and revolts. A large
part of the reign of Gustavus was occupied in struggling
against insurrections. They were caused partly by dissatisfaction with the king's ecclesiastical reforms, and
partly by the heavy taxation which he was compelled
to impose. An insurrection was attempted to be organized by the High Steward, Thuré Johnson. He
gathered a number of the leading men of West Gothland, and urged them to depose the king who had
forsaken the Christian religion, persecuted the Church,
and usurped the throne which belonged of right to
the house of Sturé. But the appeal was unsuccessful.
Johnson was compelled to flee, after having committed
some overt acts of rebellion, by which his life would
have been forfeited. Gustavus issued a decree of oblivion for all who had been implicated in this attempt

—except two prominent and leading lords. He thus, according to his usual policy, so blended mercy with severity that the dissatisfied might be intimidated, and the forgiven be led by gratitude or fear to become loyal or quiet in the future.

Diet of Strengness. At the Diet which was summoned in consequence of this insurrection Gustavus repelled the charges which were made by Johnson the pretext for rebellion. To the charge of fostering heresy he answered that it was not he but the Lord who had commanded the pure preaching of the Gospel. As to other points of doctrine he was content that learned men should meet and adjust them. He denied that he had broken his oath to preserve the privileges of the Church, for it had been decided at Westeras *what those privileges were*, and those, thus authoritatively defined, he had preserved. The old oath of subjection to the Pope and his agents he had indeed declined to take; and when he pledged himself to protect the Church he understood, and none better than Thuré Johnson knew that he understood, that he took upon himself the obligation, "to protect and uphold the Church and Churchmen, that is to say his Christian subjects, *since the Holy Church is no other than the congregation of Christian men and women.* Did any one interpret his oath as confined to bishops, prelates and priests? then let him remember that the diminution of their power was affected by the council and estates of the kingdom." The appropriation of convents to the establishment of hospitals and schools and to the urgent necessities of the Government, had proved an equal advantage to both the Church and State. It is true that he had taken many valuables from the convents when they became empty, but he had used them partly for the aid of the Government, and partly to maintain students in theology, that there might be a supply of persons qualified to teach and to preach throughout the kingdom. The Swedish Mass he had not forbidden, and the Latin Mass he had allowed to be used only in part with the Swedish; because it was more edifying for the people to hear and use language which they understood than to hear and repeat by rote an unknown tongue.

We get an insight into the deplorable previous condition of Sweden, and the overshadowing and blighting influence of the Church, from the further explanations of Gustavus in reference to the decrees of Westeras, which had been adduced as one of the great moving causes of the rebellion. The king explained fully the reasons which had led to their enactment. They had found that the worldly engagements of the bishops interfered with their duty as preachers of God's Word; their power and their strongholds with the king's rights, and the administration of justice; and were besides inconsistent with our Saviour's commands that His ministers should not be temporal princes. They had found that the estates and tenants of the convents were grossly neglected; that the monks in each had diminished from forty or fifty or sixty, to five or six; and that owing to their ample provision they were leading luxurious lives. Moreover they believed that God would be better worshiped by more preaching and less singing and reading; and that monasteries and cathedrals with a large staff of clergy were not necessary to the right performance of divine service. It also appeared from the old registers that where there had formerly been a hundred nobles, there were now only three or four; the nobles had been induced through superstition, or when hard pressed for

money, to mortgage their estates to monasteries; and
hence their descendants became peasants, and almost
all the revenues of the country were in the hands of the
clergy, who gave no personal service to the crown; and
the kingdom was deprived of those men of high birth
and large wealth who constituted the ornament and
support of the throne.

Third Re- The third and last revolt of the Dalesmen
volt of the was brought about by a cause which touched
Dalesmen. the sentiments and feelings no less than the
pockets of the sturdy and pugnacious malcontents.   It
seems that up to the year 1529 the debt due to Lubeck
had not been paid, although imposts had been laid for
the specific purpose of discharging it.   In that year it
became no longer·possible to evade the payment.   The
Lubeckers threatened to detain Swedish ships as security for the debt.   Accordingly at Orebo, in 1531, it
was agreed that, in addition to the appropriation for a
time of the tithes for that purpose, the superfluous bells
of the town and country parishes should be given up or
redeemed.

These decrees produced everywhere, and especially
in the Dales, the most intense dissatisfaction.   The
removal of the most valuable bells in a chime changed
old familiar melodies into a painful jangle, and broke
up many sacred associations which were dearer to the
people than they knew before they were destroyed.
The Swedes always have been and still are very fond
of church bells; and in many small villages in Sweden
the tourist will often be surprised at the fine tone and
sweet chimes of bells in poor and plain churches.   The
bells, moreover, had acquired something of a sacred
character by having been christened and anointed.
The removal of them caused another revolt in Dale-

carlia, which was put down with no little difficulty. The futile attempts to adjust this difficulty need not be described. The process of calling a conference, and surrounding it with soldiers, of arresting and executing the leaders of the revolt, and the renewal of pledges of obedience, were all again repeated. This was the last commotion which had any connection with ecclesiastical affairs for a number of years succeeding. The Dalesmen learned at length that they had to do with a king who would not surrender his prerogatives; who would deal sternly and even unjustly with his subjects when the safety of the State or of his throne was in question; whose prudence defeated all their schemès, and whose severity punished every outrage.

Provision for Preaching and Church Services. The most important portion of the decree of Orebo was that which enjoined that provision should be made by the bishops for the preaching of the Gospel. But Gustavus did not leave the execution of the decree to those who he well knew would not cordially enforce it. He sent one or two learned and able preachers to each diocese, to preach in the cathedrals, and to establish cathedral schools for the training of a preaching ministry. The indefatigable Olaus Petri prepared postils—corresponding to the English book of homilies—for the people, to be read by those priests who were incompetent to prepare suitable sermons of their own. He also provided a church manual in the Swedish tongue. This was not published by the authority of any church synod, but it came into general use. In this there were offices for the sick, for baptism, marriage and burial, as well as for the performance of the public services. Two years later, when the introduction of the Mass in the Swedish tongue was complained of by the Dalesmen, Olaus published a work in which he showed the propriety of this arrangement; and at the same time the office for the Swedish Mass, as it is still used in Sweden, was prepared by him. It has been noticed that no direction for preaching is given, and no place assigned for it, in the first four editions of this book. But the use of the book soon extended through the kingdom, and the point in the service where the preaching should take place was designated in 1548. The necessity for this movement and its gradual influence are thus described by the Swedish historian, Anjou:

"Of the success of a work so important to the Reformation, by acquainting the people with the Gospel and its meaning, by introducing true evangelical freedom through a true faith in the Son, who makes us truly free, we cannot expect to procure information from times yet unable to prepare workmen to cultivate the field of the church. The preaching of God's Word, the purifying of divine service from superstitions and strange practices, and from a language not understood, together with the reclaiming of the ecclesiastical constitution from being a hindrance to being a means of furthering the kingdom of God, were important steps, and the commencement of a holy progress to a holy end."

Laurentius Petri Elected Archbishop. The Metropolitan See of Upsala had been vacant for ten years. This omission to fill the most important see in Sweden probably arose, partly from the fact that the king could draw from it while vacant a large revenue, and partly from his manifestly increasing indifference, if, not repugnance, to the Episcopal constitution of the Church. Lars Anderson, his chancellor, often remonstrated with Gustavus at this delay; and this was the beginning and the cause of the alienation between them. But so great had the dissatisfaction of the country become, in consequence of this long delay, and the evils which it involved, that the king was compelled to take measures in 1530 for filling the see. The Bishop of Abo, Jno Skyette, was elected, but declined. Bishop Sven, of Skara, was elected by the Chapter of Upsala, and he also declined. In the spring of 1531 the king summoned an assembly of the bishops and the chief clergy of the kingdom to Stockholm, to elect an archbishop. Laurentius Petri was elected by a large majority. It is mentioned as an indication of the predominant Protestant sentiment of the body, that one hundred and fifty votes out of one hundred and seventy-one were cast for the well-known uncompromising champion of the Reformation, while only seven of the remaining twenty-one votes were cast for candidates who were regarded as lukewarm towards the new or secretly devoted to the old system. The new archbishop was but thirty-two years of age. For forty years he administered the see with wisdom and gentleness, and with an unswerving adherence to his Protestant principles in the midst of difficulties which arose on the one hand from the encroachments of the king on his prerogatives, and on the other from the pressure of those who desired to push the Reformation further forward.

Changes in the other Sees. After the flight of Bishop Brask the See of Linkoping was committed to Bishop Jons. After Bishop Magnus, of Skara, had abandoned his diocese it was placed under the care of its provost-master, Sven, who was subsequently elected bishop of the see. These proceedings were a practical proclamation of independence of the Pope, who, as Bishops Brask and Magnus had not resigned their sees, still regarded them as their rightful incumbents. In 1530 Jons Bethius, Canon of Wexio, became its Bishop, on the death of Bishop Ingemar. Magnus Sommer, of Strengness, and Petrus Magni, of Westeras, were all that were now left of the bishops who had approved or acquiesced in the decrees of Westeras. But when they were led to hope that, by the aid of Charles V., Christian II. might recover his three thrones, they circulated treasonable appeals to the people from the exiled Archbishop Trolle and Bishop Magnus, of Skara. The king had summoned the three bishops elect to appear at Stockholm for their consecration and his own nuptials. He had also summoned the Bishops of Strengness and Westeras to officiate at the consecration of the archbishop and the three bishops elect. Their conduct on this occasion shows that they were not the stuff of which martyrs are made. . Just before their journey to Stockholm they prepared a protestation, in which they declared their abhorrence of the soul-destroying heresy of Luther, and of the consecration of the intruded bishops and archbishop, which they were compelled unwillingly to perform "under the influence of apprehensions and fears which may well arise even in firm minds." This cowardly document was not to be made public unless a change of dynasty should make it necessary as a matter of self-defense. Whether the king knew of its existence is doubtful; but he was quite well aware of the secret disloyalty of both these prelates. Bishop Petrus retained his office until his death in 1534, and was succeeded the year after by Herrick Johannes, who became an ardent Reformer. Bishop Sommer was imprisoned by the king in 1536, was released after eight

months, but not again restored to his see. He ended
his days in the cloister of Krokek as an avowed member
of the Church of Rome, and in the undisturbed enjoyment of its faith, in the year 1543. Thus as early as
1531 the Swedish Church was completely established
in independence of the Church of Rome. All of its
bishops professed, and all but two sincerely embraced,
and earnestly propagated, the Protestant faith. But
as yet its rules of discipline were uncertain, and the
power of the king in ecclesiastical questions was practically supreme.

CHAPTER VI.

CONDITION OF THE CHURCH TO THE CLOSE OF THE REIGN OF KING GUSTAVUS.

Conspiracy against the Life of the King. DURING the five years between 1531 and 1536 Gustavus seems to have consolidated his power, and to have had some prospect of the peaceful reign for which he longed, and which he was never to enjoy. He had foiled the Lubeckers in their attempt to reinstate Christian. That tyrant was defeated and imprisoned, and no more danger was to be feared from him. The turbulent Dalesmen were thoroughly humbled and subdued, and would henceforth give him no further trouble. An heir was born to him, and thus the power to agitate the country with intrigues for the succession was much diminished. But in that moment of the seeming greatest security he was in fact in the greatest peril. A plot against his life, concocted by demagogues in Lubeck, in connection with some German burghers of Stockholm, which had remained passive while the result of the war was uncertain, was after its conclusion revived and ripened. The conspirators prepared a number of schemes for the murder of the king, to be employed in turn if it should prove to be necessary. First, a barrel of gunpowder furnished with a fuse, capable of burning three hours, was to be placed under his seat in the high church, and to be exploded during the divine service. Should this fail, Anders Hanson, the king's master of the mint, who had married a sister of Bishop Brask, was to stab him in the Treasury of Stockholm Castle. If this scheme should fail, he was to be taken off by poison. The loyal inhabitants of Stockholm were then to be murdered, and the city to be included in the Hanseatic League. On the day before that appointed for the execution of the plot, a drunken sailor, made desperate by need, was engaged to fire the train. Returning home intoxicated from a carouse with those by whom he was employed, he revealed to a neighbor and his wife what was to take place on the following day. The latter immediately sent word to the commandant of Stockholm, and before morning all the conspirators were secured and most of them executed.

The Attitude of Gustavus towards the Clergy. It is evident that Gustavus came very little under the influence of the clergy, and that he regarded them generally with dislike, and was inclined to treat them with severity when they exhibited a grasping spirit or intrigued against him. Yet he did not fail to do justice and to render honor to those who were faithful and godly men; and he himself was beyond doubt, from full conviction a sincere believer. We can scarcely wonder that such should have been his feeling, especially towards the bishops and the higher clergy, to whom all the evils and burdens of the country were due, and by whom all the rebellions that had arisen either originated or had been fostered, and from many of whom he had received only gross treachery and ingratitude in return for the favors he had heaped upon them. We can plainly trace this feeling in several incidents which occurred after the supremacy of the Reformation had become assured.

We see it in his treatment of Bishop Sommer, and of his successor, Bishop Bothvid. During the festivities connected with the king's second marriage, Bishop Sommer declared that he could no longer sanction and support the Lutheran religion. At an earlier period of his reign the king would undoubtedly have allowed him to retain his see, and would have restricted him only from the practice of those abuses and extortions by which the Roman clergy had heretofore oppressed their flocks. But upon this declaration of the bishop, made incidentally under a sudden impulse, and not intended as a formal announcement of his purpose, Gustavus immediately, without invoking the intervention or advice of his clergy, deposed him. His successor. an Evangelical Canon of Linkoping, named Bothvid, being asked by the king, who had cast a longing eye on his Episcopal palace, "In what chapter of the Bible is it written that the bishops of Strengness should live in palaces of stone?" replied, "In the same chapter that gives the kings of Sweden Church-tithes!" The repartee was bright but indiscreet, and is said well nigh to have provoked the fate of his predecessor.

The Trial and Condemnation of Lars Anderson and Olaus Petri. The strength of this feeling of hostility to the clergy on the part of Gustavus is painfully apparent from his treatment of his two nearest and most trusted friends, Anderson and Petri. Their trial and condemnation to death four years after the conspiracy, upon charges which, if proved, would not have been high treason, and the alleged proof of which was most vague and unsatisfactory, lead to the inevitable inference that it was passion and prejudice which drove the king to the commission of a great crime, which was aggravated by its gross ingratitude. These were the two friends who more than any and all others most thoroughly entered into his convictions and plans for the Reformation. The causes of his alienation from them arose from changes in himself, rather than from any deviation on their part, from the policy and proceedings which he had formerly approved. The chancellor sometimes acted with less direct reference to the king in the decisions which came within his jurisdiction than the latter, more and more bent on absorbing all power, temporal and spiritual, approved. Olaus, full of enthusiasm and zeal, sometimes uttered from the pulpit sharp reproofs, which touched Gustavus nearly, and which he could not but see were directed against him. But these were surely pardonable faults on the part of those to whom he and Sweden owed such immense obligations. The two charges upon which they were convicted by the commission appointed for their trial, were that they had been cognizant of the conspiracy which was discovered four years since and had not divulged it, because it was made known to them under the seal of the confessional, and that Olaus in the Swedish Chronicles, *which were published ten years before*, had made severe reflections which the king believed, but without probability or proof, were directed against him.

The first charge seems upon the face of it most improbable. Lars Anderson had earnestly promoted the Reformation and at an early period, at the command of the king, had translated the New Testament into Swedish, and had with great reputation filled the office of High Chancellor of the Kingdom. Olaus Petri, by his preaching and publications and the composition of the Church Manual, had vindicated the Reformation and given shape and organization to the Church. He

had also succeeded Anderson in the office of High
Chancellor. And, although a qualified confessional
was retained in the early period of the Reformed
Swedish Church, it is yet incredible that one whom
Gustavus felt to be rather too much than too little of a
Reformer and one so near and dear and devoted to the
king, from conscientious scruples which only bigoted
Romanists could entertain, had kept a secret on which
not only the life of one whom he so much honored, but
also the welfare of the kingdom and the success of the
Reformation, depended. That Gustavus, who had so
often exhibited indifference to abuse and retained his
dignity in the midst of gross misrepresentations, should
have been so stung by seeming reflections against him,
which were published ten years before, and the application of which to himself seems doubtful, shows that
a great change must have come over him, the causes
of which will presently appear. It was a most painful
incident in this mysterious trial that the Archbishop
Laurentius Petri was compelled to preside and sit in
judgment on his brother. The lives of both of the accused were spared, as it was probably the purpose of
Gustavus that they should be. But the position of Olaus
in the popular regard appears from the fact that his life
was ransomed by a large sum of money advanced for
him by the burghers of Stockholm. His vindication
also seems to have been pronounced by the people,
and virtually acquiesced in by Gustavus himself, by his
restoration three years after to the Rectorship of the
Church in Stockholm. Anderson ransomed his life at
the price of the surrender of all that he possessed. He
remained under the royal displeasure and died in poverty and obscurity.

It was a cruel proceeding—this condemnation of

those whose services to the king and the Reformation
had been so great, and whose offense, even if it had
been proved, which it was not, was not worthy of death.
It has left an ineffaceable stain upon the else luminous
and glorious record of the Great King's history. The
just and right-minded son of Gustavus, Charles IX.,
was so convinced upon examination of the innocence
of these victims of his father's injustice " that he would
not allow the charges against them to remain in the
history of his father."

Causes of the Change in the Views and Policy of the King. The growing feeling of alienation from the
clergy was greatly increased by the advent
of two foreigners into the kingdom, through
whose influence a new policy in ecclesiastical
affairs was introduced. Gustavus was led by them into
the adoption in theory and in practice of the most high-
handed Erastianism. His dislike of the Episcopate,
which was the greatest obstacle to the power of the
king in spirituals, was also inflamed into positive hostility by the same agency. It was Conrad Peutinger,
who came into Sweden from Germany in 1538, and became Cantor of the Cathedral of Upsala, who poisoned
the mind of Gustavus against Olaus Petri and Lars Anderson, and secretly put in motion the proceedings
which led to their trial and condemnation. In his project for bringing the Church of Sweden into conformity
to the Lutheran churches of Germany he found an ef-
ficient co-worker in an ordained Pomeranian noble,
George Norman, who had studied at Wittenberg, and
who also arrived in Sweden in 1538, as the tutor
of Prince Eric, heir to the Swedish throne. They dwelt
in their conversations with the king upon the differences
between the Church in Sweden and all the Lutheran
churches of Europe, and aggravated the restrictions to

which he was subjected. " The king in Sweden ought
to have the same power over the Church as was exercised by all the German princes.   Henry VIII. of England had made himself head of the Church in his kingdom.   In the constitution of the Church, bishops might
well be dispensed with, or at least limited in the exercise of their powers.   Neither Luther nor Melancthon
were bishops."   These representations fell on willing
ears.   " The king was now transformed into a Protestant in the strictest sense of the term, after the pattern
of German Lutheranism."

Depression After the condemnation of Olaus Petri and
of the Epis- Anderson, these two foreigners enjoyed the
copate. full confidence of the king, and directed the
ecclesiastical affairs of the kingdom.   Gustavus himself
adopted a harsh and angry tone towards the clergy.
He reproached them for what he called their injudicious
alterations of harmless old usages, which were dear to
the people, and whose removal excited their anger.
He signified to them that he perceived, that like the
old priesthood, they aimed to become his master.   Peutinger was advanced to the chancellorship of the kingdom, and Norman was invested with a superintendency
whose power extended to all the clergy, and made in
effect the archbishop to be under his authority and in
a sense subject to his jurisdiction.   If it were not, as
there is reason to suppose that it was, the design of
this arrangement ultimately to abolish Episcopacy, it
cannot be denied that such was its tendency, and that
its immediate effect was to depress and rob it of its old
traditional dignity and power.   The king, apparently
in imitation of Henry VIII., and employing almost
identical phraseology, announced himself as " the supreme defender of the Christian faith over the whole

realm;" and in a letter to all his bishops, prelates and other spiritual pastors and preachers, appointed George Norman as *his ordinary* and *superintendent*. Norman, with the consent of a council and assistant, was empowered to exercise the king's jurisdiction over bishops, prelates and all other spiritual persons. He was to see that all preachers should set an example of godly living to the subjects of the king. All spiritual persons were to be inducted into office by him, and his visitations were to be made at the times and places designated by the king. A board of elders who were laymen were to follow the superintendent and see that the regulations which he had prescribed were carried into effect. One of the prerogatives of the office of superintendent, the execution of which caused much clamor, was the authority to abstract from the churches as much of their ornaments and the old appliances for worship, with their gold and silver and jewels, as he should judge needful for the king's service. This new office reduced the archbishops and the bishops to insignificance and inaction. From the year 1544 the king ceased to give the Episcopal title to any of the bishops except the Archbishop of Upsala. The other bishops were called "ordinaries;" and as all jurisdiction was practically taken from them by the Superintendent and his assistants, nothing remained to them but the power of preaching and ordaining. To diminish still further their importance and their power, the sees of Upsala and of Linkoping were divided into three dioceses, and those of Westeras and Strengness each into two. This continued to be the condition and constitution of the Church in Sweden from the year 1544 to the close of his reign in 1560. From this period to the end of his reign Gustavus openly claimed absolute authority in Church and State. In a letter to the peasantry in the affair of Dieting, he thus wrote:

" Ye would wish to be far better scholars than we and many good men beside, and hold much more fast by the traitorous abuses of the old bishops and papists than by the Word and Gospel of the living God. Far be this thought from you! Tend your households, fields and meadows, wives and children, kine and sheep, *but set to us no bounds in government and religion.* Since it behooveth us a Christian monarch, for God's sake and for righteousness, conformably to all natural reason to appoint ordinances and rules for you, so that if ye would not look to have wrath and chastisement from us, ye should be obedient to our royal commandment as well in religion as in temporals."

Condition of the Church under this new ar- rangement. As the Church was settled in the form of the superintendency of a presbyter over bishops, the Archbishop of Upsala alone receiving the title of bishop, all others of that order being called ordinaries—so did it continue during the remain- der of the reign of Gustavus. The absolutism which the king had established over the Church—the open and peremptory Erastianism which he had persuaded him- self was the only method of preserving the Church from falling back into the power of the papacy—continued undiminished. In the midst of the difficulties in which Gustavus was involved, and the amazing activity which he displayed, in bringing his kingdom into an orderly administration, and in developing its resources, we can trace but few notices of the condition of the Church. Here and there we hear of an appropriation of Church or monastic property by the king, which causes loud complaints; of the efforts of the king to secure a better educated clergy; of his heavy hand laid upon the nobles;

who abused the power of reclaiming estates given to the Church since the inquest of Charles Canutson, and of the gradual decrease of the partisans of the old Church and the corresponding increase of the adherents to the new. The characteristics of the Church thus settled, most of which have continued to the present day, may thus be briefly indicated.

1. In consequence of the toleration of the Church of Rome, and of the efforts of Gustavus, while he removed its abuses, to avoid as far as possible to irritate the people by too sudden a change in the externals of worship which did not immediately involve and express superstition and error, there were retained in the Church services more of paraphernalia and ceremonialism than was usual in the Lutheran churches in countries where the Roman worship was suppressed, and Episcopacy did not obtain. The cross and crucifixes and candles and gorgeous garments in the administration of the Lord's Supper and an elaborate ritual were still maintained.

2. Another characteristic which honorably distinguishes this Church and is especially to be commended in Gustavus to whom it is due, in view of the exasperating and traitorous opposition which he endured from the partisans of the Papal Church, was the absence of persecution and the toleration of the Church which so constantly labored to overthrow both Protestantism and the king. There were no fines, punishments, imprisonments or executions for holding and openly professing the faith and practicing the ceremonies of the Roman Church. There was indeed a cutting off of its civil privileges and supremacy, a protection of the citizens and of the members of the Church itself from the extortions of the priesthood, a resumption of Church and monastic property for the uses of the State, a reduction

of the livings of the high ecclesiastics to a very narrow
allowance compared with that of former times, and a
swift and sharp punishment of treason, with no regard
to rank or priestly sanctity, when it sheltered itself under
the plea of religion, and of supreme obligation to the See
of Rome. All this would indeed be called persecution
by those whose privileges were abridged; but there
were no cruelties exercised against peaceable and loyal
members of the Church of Rome, merely because of their
adherence to the old faith. We cannot say so much of
the Lutheran Churches of Germany in their relation to
the members of the Roman and Reformed Churches, or
of the Church of England in relation to Romanists and
Puritans. Later indeed in the history of Sweden, after
prolonged and reiterated proofs of the essentially traitorous and rebellious character of Romanism, this toler-
ant policy ceased, and the public profession of Romanism was not allowed.

The Civil Ad- The secular historian of the last sixteen
ministration years of the reign of Gustavus would find
of Gustavus. in it abundant proofs of his great administrative ability, his wonderful activity, his successful efforts to stimulate the industry of the people, and develop the resources of the kingdom, and the steady
increase of veneration and admiration for him, notwithstanding much vexatious opposition to which he was
exposed from his pugnacious subjects. He would also
be compelled to admit that Gustavus became greedy
of appropriating to himself, sometimes with little or no
claim, a large share of the forfeited property of the
churches and the monasteries; and that he accumulated
in his palace a large treasure, subsequently squandered
by his half-crazy son and successor, which might have
been well employed in promoting the material and

moral welfare of the people. During the remainder of
his life there were no serious internal revolts; and but
one brief war with Russia in reference to the boundary
of Finland. In view of the enormous difficulties which
he encountered, the reign of Gustavus is one of the most
remarkable in the history of Europe, and entitles him
to a place only second to that of the few greatest monarchs—such as Alfred and Charlemagne and William
the Conqueror—who were pre-eminent in their time,
and have left the impress of their genius on all subsequent generations.

Secular and Religious Education; and the Condition of the Clergy.   Inasmuch as we have thus far dealt chiefly
with the class that have the highest educa-
cation—the clergy—and as something has
been said of the efforts of the king for the
secular and religious education of the people, a higher idea of the civilization of Sweden at this
period may be inferred than the facts will warrant.
When one narrates the public events of a country poor
and but partially civilized, or but little advanced in the
refinements of life, in the same phraseology with which
he speaks of kingdoms that are rich and cultivated, he
may convey a wrong impression without misstating
facts. It is natural to describe the public events of
Sweden and France, for instance, secular and religious,
in the same phraseology; and yet in the one case it is
the history of a comparatively poor people in whose
higher classes there was great simplicity of life and no
little remaining rudeness of manners, in the other it is
a history of a people whose aristocracy were highly
cultivated and luxurious, and surrounded with all the
appliances of a refined civilization. Hence it is important to present a sketch of the condition of education
in the kingdom, with the remark that if it does not ex-

hibit a bright picture of the national life, it still should be remembered that it shows a great advance over the state of things which prevailed previous to the reign of Gustavus.

The Schools, the Clergy, and the Peo- ple. One of the native historians of the kingdom gives this account of it, as it appeared to- wards the close of the reign of Gustavus. "The older seminaries of instruction had been too closely connected with the ancient church not to be involved in its downfall. Hvitfeld and Messenius indeed state that Gustavus in 1540 revived the University of Upsala, founded twenty years before; and two years previously we find him complaining that circumstances did not permit him to complete this work which it was his desire to accomplish. In the archives of his reign no trace of its actual performance is to be found, although they supply many proofs of the king's fostering care for the schools, which nevertheless do not appear in all respects to have answered their object if we may judge by the trenchant rêproof addressed by him to the bishops in the year preceding his deáth, relative to the character of the persons who were supplied to him by the schools for the service of the State. A learned Swede who resided abroad draws at the same time a dark picture of the condition of his country in this respect, and concludes that the large hoard of gold and silver, the military stores, the ships, the arms and the fortifi- cations were rather detrimental than profitable; inas- much as out of all the bands which the king every- where maintained, not without great cost and to the sore molestation of the subject, not ten men were to be found whose counsel he might employ in the affairs of his kingdom; and the same held true of the nobles, of the heads of the church, and of the priests.   Lieuten-

ants and persons in authority kept each of them a sec-
retary to read and answer the king's letters, as they
were themselves unable to do so. Of the rudeness and
ignorance of the clergy many proofs remain. Their
manner of embracing the principles of the Reformation often consisted only in marrying their house-
keepers, in order thereby to legitimate the offspring
which they had borne them. The evangelical ministers themselves did not always set an edifying example. The abolition of the old church discipline before
the new order of things was matured, was generally
productive of injurious effects on domestic morals. The
king, whose own life was pure, and deportment blameless, often denounces the prevailing corruption of manners. To what extent this reached where other circumstances favored the lawlessness of the ill-disposed,
as on the frontiers, is best shown by his letter to the
inhabitants of the prefecture of Kronoberg in 1554. In
this, referring probably to the visitation of 1550, he re-
proves those who, living on the borders, and moving
hither and thither, now into Denmark and now into
Sweden, are regardless of their marriage vow, and take
to wife one woman after another, as they would change
their horses. He commanded the prefects to watch
narrowly the proceedings of these loose companions.
At the same time the severity of the temporal penalties was increased till at length adultery was punished
with death.

The latter
days of Gus-
tus.
The latter days of Gustavus were darkened
by great domestic sorrows. His eldest son
Eric, the heir to the throne, a prince of great
ability, but vicious and eccentric, and excitable to a
degree little short of derangement, caused him great
trouble, and filled him with anxiety for the future of

himself and of his kingdom. The king had assigned to him the province of Calmar; and there he had exercised his authority with reckless cruelty, and surrounded himself with a gay and licentious court and plunged into revelry and excess. And that which broke the heart of the king, and sent him soon after to the grave, was the misconduct of his favorite beautiful and gifted daughter Cecelia. "The court poets," says the historian Freyxell, "praise her as lovelier than Venus; they could not sufficiently extol her white skin, her golden hair, and her sparkling eyes; and they protested that her soul was adorned with equal virtues. But she soon exhibited an incorrigible levity and vanity which led her to a guilty intrigue with Count Edgard of Friesland; and to an after-life of frequent adulteries, and of intemperance, which ended in a dishonored and disowned old age. Eric caused his father much anxiety, and great expense, in his Quixotic efforts to secure the hand of the Princess Elizabeth, afterward queen, of England. Without the slightest encouragement, and indeed in the face of emphatic dissuasives from the princess, he continued to urge his wild suit, and to send expensive embassies to England. All these domestic troubles, and especially the dishonor of his favorite daughter, broke the spirits of the old king, and brought on a decline of health and an enfeeblement of his powers of body and of mind. The loss of his beloved wife Margaret, and of many of his contemporaries, his co-workers in the task of emancipating Sweden, was not compensated by his union with a third wife, young and beautiful and excellent, Catherine Leyohnhufwud. That indeed brought with it also a new element of annoyance, from the fact that

Catherine was a niece of the late queen of Gustavus, and that his nearest friend, Archbishop Laurentius Petri, and many other ecclesiastics, denounced the marriage as incestuous and unlawful. With failing powers and with frequent deep depression, the old king, feeling that his end was near, summoned a general meeting of all the States in order to receive from them the confirmation of his last will and testament, in which he appointed Eric his successor and indicated the disposition to be made of the great wealth and the numerous estates all over the kingdom which he had acquired. The scene of that last audience of the king with his States was very impressive.

The King's last Speech to the States: and his Death. The meeting took place in the hall of audience in the palace of Stockholm on the 25th of June. When the States were assembled the king entered, leaning upon the arms of his two eldest sons. His sons Duke Eric, Duke John and Duke Magnus stood at his left hand in the order of their age; and his young son Duke Charles, still a child, stood by his knee. The king having saluted the States, they listened for the last time to the eloquence which they liked so well, that when in the Diet Gustavus deputed some one else to speak for him they were wont to cry out that they wanted to hear their father-king. Then the king spoke as follows:—

"I venerate the power of God who in me has elevated to the old throne of Sweden the old race of Sweden's kings from Magnus Laduläs and Karl Canutson. Those amongst you who have attained to many years have doubtless learned how our dear Fatherland was for many centuries before in great misery and oppression, under foreign rulers and kings, especially under the harsh tyrant King Christian, and how

it has pleased God through me to deliver us from
this tyranny. Therefore ought we, high and low, lord
and master, old and young, never to forget the same
Almighty aid. For what man was I to expel so
mighty a lord, who not only ruled over three kingdoms, but was allied and nearly connected with the
Emperor and the most powerful princes. I could not
imagine so great a glory would be mine when in forests
and among the rocks of the desert, I was obliged to
conceal myself from the sword of the blood-thirsty
enemy. But God impelled the work and made me his
instrument by whom his Omnipotence should be revealed; and I may well compare myself to David,
whom the Lord took from being a poor shepherd to
be a king over all his people—" and here the tears
burst from his eyes.

"I thank you, faithful subjects, that you have been
pleased to elevate me to the royal dignity and make
me the ancestor of your royal house. Nor less do I
thank you for the fidelity and aid you have given me
in my government. That during this time God has
permitted his pure and precious Word to enter in
among us, that also in temporal concerns he has
prospered and endowed the kingdom with all manner
of blessing as we see before our eyes; for this we
ought, good men and subjects, with the greatest hu-
mility and gratitude, to give God the glory.

"It is well known to me, that I, in the estimation of
many, have been a stern king; but the time will come
when the children of Sweden would wish to tear me
from my grave if they could do it. But I must not
blush to acknowledge human weaknesses and failings,
for none is perfect and without fault. Therefore I beg
you, that you, as faithful subjects, will for Christ's sake

forgive and overlook what errors there may have been in my government. My intentions have always been for the weal of this kingdom and its inhabitants. My gray hairs, my wrinkled brow, bear sufficient witness to the many dangers, adversities and cares, which I in the forty years of my reign have had to undergo.

"I know well that the Swedes are swift to promise, slow to execute. I can clearly see that many spirits of delusion will arise in the future; I therefore pray and exhort you to hold fast to God's Word; and reject what does not agree with it. Be obedient to your rulers and united among yourselves. My time is soon out. I neither require stars nor any other sign to prophecy that to me. I feel in my own body the tokens that I shall soon go hence, and at the foot of the King of king's lay down my account for the glorious but perishable crown of the kingdom of Sweden. Follow me therefore with your faithful prayers, and when I have laid my eyes together let my ashes rest in peace."

"With that," writes Freyxell, "he stretched out his hand for the last time blessing his people. His gray hair, his fallen, but still majestic appearance, the tears which sometime came into his eyes, his voice ever pleasant, but now tremulous with age and emotion, and finally the thought that they were about to lose him for ever—him, their father, teacher and benefactor —all combined to awaken the deepest emotions in the whole assembly. Tears streamed from every eye, and they could scarcely prevent their sobs from drowning the sound of the beloved voice. Gustavus arose and supporting himself on his two eldest sons, he left the hall, turning his head now and then, by looks and tearful eyes, to take yet a last farewell. The assembly followed closely on his traces; those who could not in person followed by their looks his gray head, with tears imploring a thousand blessings on it."

Gustavus died on the 29th of September and was buried in the cathedral of Upsala.

Description of Gustavus. Instead of the attempt to delineate the character of Gustavus, I will give almost all the chapter in which the native historian Freyxell draws a graphic picture of one of the noblest and most interesting characters in the history of modern Europe. In a work the title of which is the Reformation in Sweden, I have done little else than describe the personal career of Gustavus. Inasmuch therefore as the history of the king cannot be separated from that of the Reformation, we may with propriety —indeed we must from necessity—give a fuller account of the character of him by whom, in an exclusive sense which does not apply to any other monarch the Reformation in his country was accomplished. There is a great charm in the narrative which is here quoted—in the characteristic national simplicity of the picture and the essentially Swedish atmosphere which invests it. We see in it a true kingliness, not devoid, in its essential characteristics, of all the august accompaniments which belong to the regal state; and yet connected with a simplicity of life and manners which is usually associated only with republican institutions.

"King Gustavus I. was a tall and well made man, somewhat above six feet high. He had a firm and full body without spot or blemish, strong arms, delicate legs, small and beautiful hands and feet. His hair of a bright yellow, combed down and cut straight across from his eyebrows; forehead of a middle height with two perpendicular lines between the eyes which were blue and piercing; his nose straight and not long, red lips and roses on his cheek even in his old age. His beard, in his younger years, was brown and parted, a hand breadth long and cut straight across; in later years growing at will, till it at last reached his waist, and became hoary like his hair. As his body was faultless in every respect, any dress which he wore became him. Fortune favored him in everything which he undertook; fishing, hunting, agriculture, cattle-breeding, mining, even to casting the dice, when he could be induced to take part in it, which however was very seldom.

"As in his body so in his soul was Gustavus endowed with noble qualities. His memory was so strong that having seen a person once, after the lapse of ten or twelve years he recognized him again at first sight. The road he had once traveled he could never mistake again; he knew the names of the villages; nay even the names of the persons who lived there during his youthful excursions. As was his memory such was also his understanding. When he saw a painting, sculpture, or architecture, he could immediately and acutely judge its merits and defects, though he had never himself received any instruction in those arts.

"When there was a crowd of people at the palace he spoke with each and on the subjects which those he addressed best understood. No man in the kingdom was so well acquainted with it as himself; none knew as well as he did in what its deficiencies lay. For this reason, and because in the beginning he was entirely without well informed and capable officers, he was obliged himself to compose every ordinance and de-cree which he enacted, and the kingdom was not a loser by it.

"Firmness and perseverance in what he undertook were striking features of his character. Example sufficient of this we find in his long, vehement, but honestly conducted, struggle with the power of Popery. Most others would have wearied or desired by a blow to decide the matter by violence. Gustavus let time and reflection work for him; though slowly he went ever forward. Seldom or never did he change his resolution; it was an adage of his which he often repeated: 'Better say once and remain by it than speak a hundred times.'

"He was a stern and serious gentleman and well knew how to preserve his dignity. It was not advisable for any, whether high or low, to encroach upon it; in such circumstances he rebuked peasants, bishops or kings with equal severity. He was just but severe with the men whom he had placed in civil charges; on which account many abandoned him. When any one labored to show off his talents and capabilities in the hope of ingratiating himself or others, or commenced to extol such an one, the sharp-sighted king would answer: 'He is but a dabbler with all his pound from our Lord.'

"Gustavus was careful of money; for he said it costs the sweat and labor of his subjects. His court was very frugal. He generally lived at one or other of the royal estates and consumed their produce. His children were kept strictly. Hams and butter were sent from the country for the supper of the princes in Upsala; the queen herself sewed their shirts, and it was considered a great present if one of the princesses got a blank Ricks thaler. Gustavus's love of money seduced him into several injustices, which however in those days were not so striking as they would be now. He sometimes permitted parishes to remain without rectors, having them administered by vicars, and appro-

priated their returns to himself.   He forbade the export
of cattle to his subjects in general, buying them at a
low price from the peasants, and selling them abroad
at a great profit.   This last circumstance was one of
the chief causes of the Dacke or peasants' revolt.
Several things of this kind which are not creditable to
him are related; but the people overlooked them for
the sake of his many virtues.   They knew also that
this money was not uselessly squandered.   Herr Eskills
Hall and the other vaulted chambers of the treasury
were full of good silver bullion at the king's death.
When however pomp was required he did not spare,
but showed himself the equal of other kings.   The
Lord's Anointed he said should be girded with splendor,
that the commonalty may view him with reverence and
not imagine themselves to be the equals of majesty to
the small profit of the land.

"A pure and unaffected piety dwelt in his heart
and showed itself in his actions.   Prayers were read
morning and evening in his apartments; divine service
he never neglected.   He was better informed of the
contents of the Bible and catechism than the most of
the priests in his kingdom.   Therefore Le Palm, his
chief physician, wrote of him to Paris: 'My king is a
God's prince who has scarce his equal in spiritual and
temporal measure.   He is so experienced in Scripture,
that he can rectify his priests, and none understands
the government of the kingdom like himself.'   During
the Dacke revolt Gustavus wrote to the rebels: 'Ye can
threaten us much as ye will; ye can drive us from our
royal throne; rob us of estate, wife, and children; aye,
of life itself; but from that knowledge which we have
attained of God's Word ye shall never part us as long
as our heart is whole and our blood warm.'

"He was equally venerable in his domestic life. No vice stains his memory. He liked the society of handsome and agreeable women; but no mistress, no illegitimate child, not the slightest foible, can be laid to his charge, though he was forty-one before he married for the first time. His marriage vows he kept inviolate. Gluttony, drunkenness, gambling, and idleness were what he could never endure in others, much less in himself.

"As he in his younger years was of a cheerful temper, when business was done, he kept a gay and lively court, though in all sobriety. Every afternoon at a certain hour the lords and ladies assembled in the great hall where the king's musicians made music for them while they danced. 'For,' said he, 'youth should not be clownish but gallant to the ladies and to all.' They were often out together to walk or to hunt; once a week a school for fencing was open for the young nobles; tournaments were afterwards introduced, at which the victors received their rewards at the hands of the fairest of the ladies. They often entertained themselves with music, with song as well as playing on stringed instruments, the latter especially in which the king delighted. He made and himself played several instruments, of which the lute was his favorite. There was never an evening when he was alone that he did not occupy some hours with it.

"He often traveled through the country, chiefly to great markets and other meetings where he addressed the people; sometimes instructing them in matters of faith; sometimes regarding their housekeeping, agriculture, cattle-breeding, and so on. The peasants soon learned that the king's advice was good and listened to him willingly; also on account of his extraordinary

eloquence.   His voice was strong, clear, and expressive
in sound.   No king of Sweden ever was, or deserved to
be , more beloved by the common people, than he was.
Any peasants who possessed any fortune used to leave
y will some silver to the king, so that at his death no
considerable store of bequeathed silver was found in
the treasury; and in the unquiet years which followed
the people ever used to speak with regret of OLD
KING GUSTAF and his happy days.

"Gustavus loved and protected learning.   He was,
however, supremely desirous of the instruction of the
people, and sought by every means to get a sensible
and well-informed peasantry.   His own children received a careful education; so that they were among
the most learned of their day.   Like his children were
the whole Wasa dynasty as far as Christina; so that
the royal house was the first, not only in pomp and
bravery; but likewise in science and knowledge; and
in this last respect not only in Sweden but in all
Europe.

"When the king grew older and his children were
growing up, he used often, after meals, to sit before the
fire and, conversing with them, give them useful exhortations on many points.   It was a royal school in
its teacher, discipline, and doctrines.   'Be steady in
your faith and united among yourselves,' said he.   'If
you fail in the first you anger your Maker; if you neg-
t the second you will fall a prey to man.   Make war
compulsion—peace without compulsion—but should
ur neighbor threaten—strike.   From my very child-
od and ever since I have been at war: oftenest with
my countrymen—sad to say!   And I have grown gray
in armor.   Believe me, seek peace with all!'   Many
other and salutary counsels follow—but enough are

here given to show his character and his sagacity. I think it will be difficult to find anywhere a nobler picture of a true father-king; or one in which we can point to so few deficiencies and faults."

Manners and Customs of the Time of Gustavus. A complete idea of the work of Gustavus in Sweden cannot well be conceived, without a sketch of the manners and customs of the time in which he lived. This also is taken unchanged from the same historian, Freyxell.

" Frugality and simplicity in everyday life; pomp, often both tasteless and ridiculous, on solemn occasions—such were the marks of the times. Many of our conveniences were wanting; glass was very rare; and instead of the wooden shutters once in use, fine net work, linen, or parchment, was now taken to supply their place. Hearths instead of stoves were used for a couple of hundred of years longer. Carpets, very coarse for the poor, embroidered with gold and silk for the rich, covered the coarsely timbered walls. Thick benches were attached to them around the room, oaken in the houses of the rich. Before them stood long heavy tables, and small stools moved about the room. Plates were scarce and were never changed, if the dishes were never so many and so various. Every guest had to bring his knife, fork, and spoon with him. Clocks were so rare that when the Grand Duke of Muscovy received one as a present from the king of Denmark, he thought it must be an enchanted animal sent for the ruin of himself and his kingdom, wherefore he returned it with the utmost dispatch to Copenhagen. Dinner was eaten at ten, supper at five; between nine and ten they went to bed, to rise the earlier in the morning. Wearing apparel was mostly woolen; linen was rarely used next the skin. Holiday dresses were costly but substantial; the same petticoat often served in succession mother, daughter, and grand-daughter, on festal occasions. The women had their hair combed back and long tight-fitting gowns with stiff high ruffles. The men wore the Spanish dress. Their hair was in the beginning long and their beard shaved; but this was soon changed, so that the clergy alone retained the long hair and the smooth skin; the others adopted short hair and long beard. Wax lights were used only in churches, tallow candles by the richest and greatest, torches of dry wood by the people. The beds were broad, fastened to the wall, and few in number; the guests were laid several together, often with the host himself. This was the case even in the houses of princes. The roads were so bad that carriages could seldom be used; besides, the first coach was not introduced until the reign of John III. Most journeys took place on horseback, and when it rained the princes were wrapped in wax-cloth cloaks. High titles were not in use. The king was called *His Grace;* the princes *Yunker Young Lord,* the princesses *Fröken,* young ladies. The nobles did not use their family but their fathers' name. There was much of savage wildness and disorder yet among the people, partly on account of· the times and the long domestic broils. Club law was more resorted to than the law of the land. Arms were in continual wear and exercise. According to an old custom the knights entered the bridal bed in full armor; but, like the knights of old, they were generally ignorant in the highest degree, especially the elder among them. Many of King Gustavus's officers and governors were unable to read, still less to write; they were obliged to keep a clerk on purpose to read and answer the king's letters. The Romish faith was done away with, but many of its superstitions remained, and that not alone among the people, but even the great ones of the land believed in witchcraft, fairies, elves, brownies, etc. The art of medicine consisted chiefly in prayers and exorcisms."

Gustavus re- peats the Mistake of Charle- magne. There is a singular resemblance in the personal character of Gustavus and Charlemagne. It is by no means certain that if the former had occupied as wide a sphere as the latter he would not have exhibited as great gifts of organization and administration. And, in the case of both, it seems remarkable that men so sagacious and experienced should have committed the fatal mistake of assigning the government of large principalities to their younger sons which rendered them in combination more powerful, though with less lofty titles, than the heir who succeeded to the throne and name of king. In both cases this mistaken policy was the cause of subsequent civil wars and convulsions, which arrested the kingdoms in which it was adopted in the path of improvement, upon which they were rapidly advancing. We shall find in this proceeding an explanation of the fact that during the reign of Eric there is scarcely anything that can be called Church History; although the events of that troubled era led to that Counter-Reformation which, with· vague and vacillating policy, was introduced by king John, the successor of Eric, and counteracted by *his* successor, king Charles. In order, therefore, to comprehend the events for which his reign prepared the way, we must trace an outline of Eric's stormy and guilty and tragic life. I leave, for a time, almost entirely, Church History; and give myself to the narration of events which verified the saying of the old king, that although he had been regarded as a stern ruler, the time would come when the children of Sweden would wish to tear him from his grave. But although the narrative is not Church History it is that without which the Church History which followed could not be understood.

CHAPTER VII.

A BRIEF mention has already been made of the dark side of Eric's character. But that mere allusion furnishes a very imperfect idea of his character as a whole. In his boyhood he gave the promise of an exceptionally gifted and brilliant manhood. He inherited from his stalwart father a handsome and vigorous *physique*. As a youth he was equaled by few of his companions in racing, swimming, and dancing, in tournaments, and in all feats of agility. " It was a pleasure," says his biographer, " but a fearful one, to see him careering on horseback."

His mental gifts, his literary accomplishments, and his solid learning, were quite beyond those of his companions of the nobility, and not often surpassed by professional scholars. He wrote and spoke Latin correctly and readily; he was skilled in astronomy and mathematics; and—unfortunately for his peace of mind—in astrology. He was, like his father, a lover and composer of music; and his poetry in Swedish was counted the best of his day. In view of his subsequent career and his crimes it seems singular to learn that two of his hymns and two of his penitential psalms are included in the Swedish Psalm book. His first tutor was Geo. Normann, who was sent to Sweden by Luther. He subsequently had

for his tutors two men who exercised a very deleterious
influence upon his excitable and impressible character.
Burraeus, a Frenchman, first put into his mind the
ambition to marry Elizabeth of England; and Goran
Persson was his evil genius, stimulating his suspicious
temper, and prompting him to deeds of cruelty throughout all his unhappy reign.

All the eminent gifts and advantages with which
Eric was endowed were neutralized by his unhappy
temperament. He was passionate, suspicious, capricious, and devoted to pleasure with a mad eagerness that
seemed almost insanity. These high excitements were
often followed by deep and moody melancholy. His
suspicion and dislike was, at an early period, excited
against his brother John by the evident, and indeed the
inevitable, preference of Gustavus for him, as the son of
his beloved Margaret, and one in whose purity, steadiness, and force of character he placed more confidence
than his subsequent history showed him to have deserved.

Patrimonies assigned to the Sons of Gustavus. The partiality of Gustavus for his son John
led him to make over to him, at the close
of the successful war with Russia, the province of Finland as his permanent patrimony.
He was induced to take this step no doubt in part by
his knowledge of the violent character of Eric, and his
conviction that his sons would receive hard measure
from him, if they were not placed in positions of independence. Finland was altogether the largest and
most important province of the kingdom. As a treaty
was set on foot for the marriage of John with a Polish
princess, Eric not unnaturally suspected that his father
was preparing to set him aside and to place his brother
upon the throne. He therefore demanded that to him
also a province of the kingdom should be assigned. The

king's want of confidence in him was shown by the fact
that he demanded that he should take a solemn oath
not to engage in any enterprise against him. That the
king was led into this fatal policy of creating his sons
dukes of such extensive provinces of his kingdom, as
to leave but a mutilated and enfeebled state for the
government of the king, through his partiality for John
and his distrust of Eric, can scarcely be doubted. For
when he had taken the one injudicious step of giving
to John so large a patrimony, it was evident that he
could withhold a similar gift from his other sons only at
the risk of their rebellion and civil war. Moreover the
same reason which induced him to take this step in the
case of John operated with equal force in the case of his
other sons. He therefore appointed Eric to be Duke
of Calmar; Magnus to be Duke of East Gothland; and
Charles, yet a youth, to be Duke of Suthermanland.
But the conduct of Eric in his government of Calmar
gave the king great uneasiness. He was surrounded
with those selfish flatterers who always gather about
and foster the vices of an heir to a throne with a view
to their own subsequent advancement. They excited
in his mind suspicions of the designs of his father and
jealousy of his brother John. Eric set spies about his
father, and the old king's lamentations over the irregularities of his son, and the painful misgivings which
he expressed as to the future of the kingdom, were
reported and exaggerated to Eric, and led to angry
and mutual reproaches. Indeed, so distressed was Gustavus with the unfilial conduct, and the suspicious measures, and the extravagant and dissipated life of Eric,
that he seriously meditated committing him to prison
and declaring Duke John heir to the throne. But after
much hesitation he finally, in his will, assigned the

throne to Eric, and the three provinces already mentioned to his three younger sons.

Dissensions between Eric and the Dukes. It was inevitable that such an arrangement as that of Gustavus's should lead to differences and dissensions. They were all the more certain to take place, that there were no definitions of the power of the king on the one hand, and the privileges of the dukes on the other. With Magnus and Charles these collisions were less likely to occur; because Charles was yet a minor, and not in possession of his dukedom; and Magnus, though violent in temper, was so weak in mind as to be readily controlled by Eric. But immediately on the death of Gustavus John wrote to his brother regarding the fulfillment of the provisions of their father's will. "It had been sufficiently known," he wrote, "how assiduous and industrious their departed father had been in gathering substance for his children; yet was there in his last will nothing determined, either in respect to the wealth he had left in cash or movables, or his many desirable estates, which now were their rightful heritage, though the deceased king had allowed these estates to flow into the treasury of the realm; he hoped that all this would now turn out to their common advantage."

Eric evaded a reply to these suggestions, and prepared to bring Duke John and his patrimony under his direct control. No sooner was Gustavus dead than Eric dispatched a messenger to Finland, to secure its pledge of allegiance to his authority. The messenger was secretly dispatched; but the knowledge of it was almost immediately conveyed to Duke John. He therefore immediately dispatched another messenger who was to ride night and day with peremptory orders to the governor of Abo not to allow the messenger of Eric to fulfill his errand. The Duke was successful in baffling the king on this occasion; but it was not long before the latter accomplished his object much more thoroughly than he could have done by his mere personal command. In the Diet of Arboga in 1561 the Estates, at the suggestion of Eric, passed a decree which precisely defined the rights of the king over the dukes, and designated the limitations of their authority. The dukes were compelled to submit to the conditions thus imposed, though they protested that many of the provisions of the act covered traps and snares of which the king might at any time take advantage for their destruction.

Those conditions are stated in full in Puffendorf's History of Sweden; and they are such as placed the brothers in absolute subjection to the king. If either of them should plot against the king's government or life he should forfeit his right of succession to the throne. If any of the subjects of the principalities should offend the king, his officers could seize upon them and they should be tried by the king's courts. Neither of the princes should come to the court with more than one hundred men. They should not engage in war without his consent; nor coin money; nor establish bishoprics. These were the main provisions established by the diet; but there were many minor ones which must have been offensive to the sense of dignity and personal honor on the part of the princes. Their real and intended purport was to defeat the purposes for which Gustavus had bestowed upon them the government of the principalities.

No less successful was Eric in his plan to deprive his brothers of a share in the possessions of their father. The dukes were limited to those possessions which had been bestowed upon them by their father previous to his death. When the estates were to be divided the king declared "that his father had unjustly regarded the land taken back from churches and convents as private property. They had been given away by former kings; therefore when restored at the perquisition were to be considered as belonging to the crown and not to the king; for which reason the royal children could have no right to them by inheritance. He therefore appropriated these estates to himself as belonging to the crown."

Thus early did the king inflame the animosity of his brothers by completely baffling their hopes, depriving them of their rights, and inflicting upon them grievous wrongs.

Coronation and Policy of King Eric. The coronation of Eric was performed with a splendor hitherto unknown in Sweden. He expended large sums from the great treasure left by Gustavus in securing from Holland a royal paraphernalia equal in magnificence and expense to that of the greatest monarchs in Europe. Feeling that his supremacy and superiority as king was not a little diminished by the fact that the dukes, his brothers, in their respective governments, occupied an independent position, and seemed rather his rivals than his lieges, Eric determined to create a small body of higher nobility who should approach to the dukes in rank and honor; and thus by diminishing the relative superiority of the dukes to all his other subjects, would place himself in a position conspicuously pre-eminent above them all. This new order of nobility he called counts. Only three members of the oldest and most famous nobility received this title. The object of Eric was apparent, and evidently intended to be so, from the method in which this new honor was conferred. As Eric placed the coronets upon the heads of the new counts the proclamation of the herald contained these sentences: "Let it be known to all that there is one king in the kingdom of Sweden and Gothland, whom God has given us and whom we see before our eyes; the most high and puissant prince and lord, Eric XIV.; and though several crowns glitter before your eyes, let none take it as if there were more than one royal crown; for, according to royal custom, royal majesty has permitted each rank, counts and barons as well as dukes, to be honored by their marks of distinction. But the king of Sweden, of the Goths and Vandals, is one and no more." The meaning of all this is evident enough. The king reminds the dukes that they, equally with counts and barons, depend upon him, notwithstanding the assignment of their patrimonies by Gustavus, for their lordships and honors. It involves the claim that they hold their positions by his tacit renewal of their father's gift; and that they are to govern their states in subordination to him.

Further Measures to strengthen the Crown. The creation of this new order of nobility, and other measures adopted to strengthen the crown, prove that if Eric had possessed steadiness and uprightness of character, his political ability and skill would have enabled him to have made his reign prosperous and renowned. His sagacity was exhibited by the establishment of a supreme court—a court of appeals from the courts of the several provinces; which was also a court of supreme original jurisdiction in every part of the kingdom. We have seen that when Sweden was subject to Denmark the effect of the non-residence of the king, and the appointment of governors for the provinces, was to give great power to those governors, and to break up the kingdom into several almost independent principalities. Under these circumstances a real, organic unity was impossible. No measure could have been better devised to give a practical unity to the kingdom, and to secure the centralization of authority in the crown, than the institution of this supreme court.

Other salutary enactments signalize the outset of the reign of Eric. A regulation has prevailed in Sweden from the time of Gustavus to the present, that the farmers and residents upon the roads were to furnish horses and entertainment for travelers at prices fixed by government. This regulation bore hard upon the rural population and the little villages of Sweden; and one of the earliest regulations of Eric was that there should be taverns or guest houses established along the post-roads to relieve the people from the obligation to entertain travelers. He also abolished several fast days, and some superstitious ceremonies still observed in the celebration of the Lord's Supper. He also proclaimed that he threw open his kingdom to all oppressed and persecuted Protestants. This brought many Calvinists into his kingdom; and Eric himself was known to prefer the Reformed to the Lutheran Church.

one Eric's
ous Mat.
tonial
S   nes.

Eric was just about to set off for England and woo Elizabeth in person when his father died. In 1561 he wrote to his envoy in London that he had again resolved to make the journey to England. Since his first proposals he had become a king and she queen of England, but the probability of her accepting him now was less even than it was before. Most extravagant were the preparations which he made for the journey. For his own display on his arrival in England he had sent on a company "of

pearl broiderers, tailors and others." As a present to
the queen he had forwarded eighteen piebald horses and
several chests of uncoined gold and silver. He embarked
in a fleet from Effsborg; but was compelled to put back
by a violent storm and did not again resume the journey. But while his envoy was prosecuting his hopeless
suit with Elizabeth he also sent a secret agent to Scotland, with an offer of his hand to Mary Queen of Scots.
While these two suits were urged at the same time, he
became so enraged with the Earl of Leicester, on hearing that he was the favorite lover of the queen, that
he directed his envoy to bribe the English Council
with money, and to secure the assassination of the
earl. At the same time he makes an offer to Renata
of Lorraine and to Christina, daughter of the Landgrave
of Hesse. With six strings to his bow, and all of them
golden, it seemed as if he might soon secure a bride.
But, notwithstanding his lavish expenditure, there seems
to have been under the elaborate courtesies with which
his proposals were received and considered, a misgiving and indisposition to yield consent, which may perhaps have arisen from rumors of his extravagant, capricious, and cruel character.

The Mar-
riage of
Duke John.
The marriage of Duke John with a Polish
princess became the cause or the occasion
of that anti-reformation which was undertaken by him when he became king, and which was
resisted and at length put down by his brother Charles.
Eric had obtained a foothold in Livonia, on the southern shore of the Gulf of Finland; and as it was likely
to be contested by Poland, he was at first reluctant to
sanction Duke John's application for the hand of Catherine Jagellonica, sister of Sigismund, King of Poland.
He was however at length persuaded to give his con-

sent. But the project was embarrassed and almost broken up by the vascillation of both the kings, Sigismund and Eric. King Sigismund insisted that as his sister Anna was the older she should be the bride; but the duke much preferred Catherine, and Catherine was sincerely attached to the duke. King Eric after he had given his consent revoked it and recalled his brother. The duke hesitated and prepared to return, but finally concluded to disobey the king. The wedding was celebrated in secret and Duke John and his bride received, on their journey to Abo, ominous intimations of the displeasure of the king. Immediately on his arrival he sent to invite the king to his wedding festivities. "But," says an historian of these events, "another feast was waiting him."

Quarrel between King Eric and the John. The suspicion and enmity of Eric against his brother John was greatly aggravated by his marriage with the Polish princess. His astrological studies had led him to the conclusion that a light-haired man would deprive him of his throne; and this he thought pointed to his brother. His pernicious counselor Goran Persson persuaded him that this marriage was the seal of a compact between Duke John against himself; and for the establishment of John and Sigismund upon the throne, and the introduction of the Roman religion into Sweden. The duke became exasperated by the evident enmity of the king; and, throwing aside all prudence and reserve, he denounced his brother at a meeting of the States of Finland, with a violence which could have no other result than open war, and which seemed to countenance the report that he had determined upon a struggle with his brother for the throne. He accused Eric of being angry because Catherine had rejected his suit and accepted himself. Eric he said had no right to Livonia—which belonged to the King of Poland. He despised the old and wise senators to whom his father was wont to resort for counsel, and was now under the sway of low and cunning adventurers, who were bringing ruin upon the kingdom. He had made so many enemies that he could neither defend his own dominions nor protect Finland from the threatened inroads of the Russians. He therefore appealed to the Fins to aid him against Eric; and declared that he had made a marriage with a sister of the king of Poland in order that by his aid he might help his unhappy country. This certainly looked like a purpose of revolt, and led to the inevitable inference that John sought to supplant his brother upon the throne.

Trial, Condemnation and Arrest of Duke John. The king did not delay to take measures to defeat his brother's schemes. Witnesses against John were everywhere sought for; and his servants were examined by torture. One of them, under the agony which he suffered, testified that "John's intention was to remove Eric from the throne." This was claimed to be perfectly satisfactory testimony. The States were summoned, the duke tried and condemned to death, as guilty of high treason. The same sentence was passed on his partisans. Those of them who could then be secured were beheaded. The sentence of the States was dispatched to Abo by Hogenskild Bijelke, who was accompanied with a considerable military force. The offer was made to John, in the king's name, that if he would surrender without resistance his life should be spared, though he would be kept in perpetual imprisonment. The duke preferred to defend himself, and stood a siege for two months, in the hope that he would be relieved by Poland. After their capture the duke and duchess were embarked upon Eric's fleet and carried to Sweden. At Waxholm, Persson went into the vessel which conveyed the duke, and made a long speech to him concerning his guilt and the proofs upon which his condemnation was pronounced. He then presented himself to the duchess, and announced to her that she would be permitted, if she desired, to live at one of the king's castles, with her ladies and a suitable maintenance; or that if she wished to accompany the duke to prison she would be permitted to do so, but would be allowed to take but two of her maids with her. The duchess, who proved herself at this time, and subsequently, to be a woman of noble character, drew off from her finger the ring of her betrothal, and held it up to Persson, saying, "Read what stands there!" The motto of the ring was *Nemo nisi mors*. "I will abide by it," exclaimed the duchess, and she did so.

The Duke's Imprison- ment. The duke was conveyed to the castle of Gripsholm not far from Stockholm. More than a hundred of his dependents and partisans were beheaded. Their bodies were exposed, some nailed to gibbets, and some left upon the rocks to be devoured by animals and birds. The old horrors of the days of the tyrant Christian seemed about to be renewed. What was to be the fate of John was yet undetermined. Eric had promised that his life should be saved if he would surrender; but the condition seemed to imply that it would be forfeited if he should resist. The king had kept himself at a distance, on the Danish frontier, where he was making preparations for war, while these frightful scenes were in progress. The brothers and sisters and all the relatives of the duke pleaded with Eric for his life, but received no hope from his answers. And yet he had not fully made up his mind. On the one hand Persson advised the duke's death, and on the other hand it was represented to him that such a proceeding would make enemies of all his kin and awaken sympathy and indignation among the people. After much vascillation the king decided that his life should be spared, but that he should suffer perpetual imprisonment. He was treated in prison with mildness and respect. The castle in which they were confined had a beautiful outlook upon the fine bay of Gripsholm and the surrounding country; and the prisoners were allowed books and writing materials and musical instruments; and the duchess was allowed with an escort to walk in the gardens of the castle.

The Insanity of Duke Magnus. I copy the account of the causes and manifestations of the insanity of Duke Magnus from the picturesque pages of the historian Freyxell. "When the death-warrant of Duke John had been made out the signature of Duke Magnus was necessary for its completion; and though weak and wavering of character it proved a most arduous undertaking to persuade him. Goran Persson, Bijekle and Beurreus traveled to and fro on this commission; they flattered and caressed the weak prince; Eric at the Diet caused the order of succession to be removed from John to Magnus; he appointed a rich and magnificent court for him; and flattered him with the hope of the lovely Mary Stuart, to whom several embassies were sent on this account. Thus seduced and stormed on every side Magnus at length gave way; but from that day forward he never enjoyed a happy hour. He was consumed by continual remorse and looked upon himself as a fratricide. His mind was unequal to these tortures and they made him at last insane. During this time he lived in Kongsbro in East Gothland, where the Motala River runs into Lake Roxen. There he often fancied that he saw a fair water nymph raise herself from the waves, and begin a song so sweet that he is said to have thrown himself from the lofty turret into the midst of the lake. He was fortunately uninjured and the guardians got him up again. This incident has given rise to a song which has been sung all over Sweden; its version, however, says that the water-nymph had frenzied Magnus by her sorcery, as a punishment for his not choosing to dwell with her. Another reason was given by the Jesuit Possevinus, who was in Sweden at a later period. He affirmed that Magnus had been struck with madness because he attempted to drive out the nuns from the convent of Wadstena. The unfortunate prince remained in this lamentable condition the rest of his life, or forty-two years more. He was buried in the Church of Wadstena."

Eric's Administration of the Kingdom. During the period of three years and more which follow the imprisonment of John the faults of Eric were more and more developed, and the condition of the kingdom became constantly more deplorable. His government was that of a suspicious and cruel tyrant who offered large rewards to informers. A court, called the Royal Court, was established, in which the doctrine of constructive or inferential treason, deduced from the most trivial incidents and expressions, led to the condemnation and death of many innocent persons. A war with Denmark and one with Norway, carried on with alternate disaster and success during these years, but with no solid ultimate advantages, exhausted the resources

of the State, and led to merciless conscriptions. When
his measures were resisted or appealed from, in any
portion of the country, the king visited those who
presumed to remonstrate and object with a ferocity
of revenge which it is scarce an exaggeration to designate as fiendish. In the few years that had elapsed
since the death of Gustavus it seemed as if all that he
had accomplished, with so much labor through many
years, for the liberty and prosperity of Sweden had
been undone; and that the unhappy country was suffering again all the evils which it experienced under
Christian, with the aggravation that they were inflicted
by a native king, and that king the son of the honored
liberator and father of their country.

Eric's Treat-
ment of the
Noble Fam-
ilies.
But while the king's general policy was ruin-
ing the country and could not have been
tolerated many years, it was his insane treatment of the Sturés and other great families
that was the immediate occasion of the measures which
led to his overthrow. The Sturés were the most eminent and worthy and beloved of all the great houses in
Sweden. The head of the family, bearing the old his-
toric name of Swante Sturé, associated with the heroic
period of Sweden's struggle for emancipation from
Denmark, was a venerable and honorable old man,
the father of a group of sons whose character sustained the well-won reputation of the house. Nils or
Nicholas, the eldest son, was distinguished for his
beauty and learning and accomplishments, and greatly
beloved for his manliness and amiability. Because of
his high reputation, connected with the fact that he
had light hair, so light as to be almost white, Eric conceived a hatred and dread of him which it was impossible
for him to conceal. The prophecy of the stars was ever

haunting him. "That white head," he said, "will bring me mischief in the end." Nils left the court in consequence of this evident hatred and suspicion, and joined the army. But even there he was surrounded by spies, and subjected falsely to the charge of having so languidly conducted a military siege as to prove that he had an understanding with the enemy. He was recalled to the court and received by the king with feigned kindness; but after three days' residence in the capital he was arrested by Persson and proclaimed a traitor by heralds riding through the streets. He was then offered the alternative of a trial by the criminal court with closed doors, or of being led through the streets mounted on a cart-horse and with a crown of straw, to symbolize his alleged aspirations to the throne. He chose to be tried, and was condemned to death and to the confiscation of his property, unless the king should extend to him his pardon. Eric's so-called clemency commuted his punishment to a degrading procession. It was carried out with every aggravation of insult and humiliation which the malice of Persson could invent.

But the effect of this cruel indignity on the army and the people was such as to warn the king to retrace his steps, if he would not himself be the instrument of advancing his supposed rival to the throne. Scarcely a week had elapsed when the king sent a messenger to Nils desiring him to proceed to Lotringen as embassador for the hand of the Princess Renata. He answered "that it was his duty to obey the king's command, but he thought that such a disgraced and dishonored man was little fitted to be a suitor in the king's name." Eric replied that "the procession had taken place by the influence of evil men, and that he would now become a gracious master to him." No doubt Nils Sturé was glad to escape from the kingdom; and he accepted the commission. He wrote to his parents: "I drank a draught at Stockholm which has crushed sense, joy, and all my welfare in this world; but I hope one day to be able to defend myself with other than letter and seal."

An alleged Conspiracy against Eric. Nothing certainly could have been more calculated to bring about a conspiracy than the infatuated proceedings of the king. But the historians of Sweden deny that there was any organized conspiracy. Dissatisfaction, murmurs and threats of revenge were no doubt heard in the households of Eric's victims. And those victims multiplied every day. He felt that the outrage upon the Sturés never could be forgiven. He lived in constant fever of alarm, augmented his body-guard, and multiplied his spies. Reports of examinations by torture and of executions by night spread terror among the people. The most trivial and innocent acts were construed by his distempered fancy into evidences of a design to murder him. The whole force and activity of the government was employed and absorbed in the search for proofs of treason. A meeting of the States was called at Swartsoe where the king was then sojourning. The nobles who were his intended victims, unconscious of their coming doom, were summoned to the Diet. A few of those who were to be accused, who were the most eminent men in the kingdom, were arrested, as also the mother of the Sturés. When Swante Sturé, coming late to the council, heard of their arrest, he took the sacrament at a small church near Swartsoe, and prepared his mind for the worst. Upon the arrest of the nobles the king announced that the Diet would be transferred to Upsala, and its numbers increased, in order that there might be a trial of the accused suited to their rank and dignity. The detestation and horror with which Eric was regarded appears from the fact that when he reached the wharf, and proceeded to the castle at Upsala, he was deserted by all his servants and arrived alone and on foot and was welcomed only by the archbishop, Lawrence Peterson, and the chancellor, Nicholas Gillenstierna.

The Diet was held on the 19th of May, 1567. Eric had been drinking excessively on the preceding day and the speech which he had prepared could not be found, and had been abstracted, as is supposed, by Persson, in the hope that in the excitement of an extemporary discourse, with shattered nerves, he would speak with more violence than he would from a carefully written address. They were not disappointed. In a vehement harangue he ran into invectives against Nils Sturé, and accused him of accumulating large treasure with a view to a revolutionary movement. The speech was received with loud murmurs of dissent, which became so alarming that the Diet was adjourned. Eric did not again personally appear in it. But the prosecution of the accused lords was pushed forward by Persson.

The proofs adduced to convict the accused of a conspiracy to dethrone the king were vague and scanty. They were inferences from expressions of indignation against the treatment of Nils Sturé and from prophecies that the king would suffer for his cruelty. Only four witnesses came forward with these statements, and two of these, after the trial, mutually accused each other of having borne false witness. Never were valuable lives sacrificed upon such flimsy testimony. It is a strong evidence of the state of feeling among the peo-

ple, that so little and such worthless testimony only
could be procured. Tyrants can generally secure any
needful amount of perjured testimony. But it is also
as strong an evidence of the subservience of diets and
legislatures in countries where all honors depend upon
a king, that this testimony was received and admitted
to be true and sufficient by all the states, or orders, except that of the clergy under the lead of their intrepid
archbishop, Laurentius Petri.

The Murder The events which followed would have fur-
of the Sturés. nished materials for tragic scenes, in the
hands of Shakespeare, equal in horror to those de-
picted in Macbeth. On the 24th of May Eric proceeded to the prison where the lords were confined
and entering the cell first of Sten Lejonhufwud and afterwards of Swante Sturé he fell upon his knees before them begging their forgiveness and promising them
their freedom. It is impossible to know whether this
was mere hypocritical acting or remorse, or a mixture
of both; but the two lords were not slow to express
their full forgiveness. Eric went so far, in his humiliation, as to request of Swante Sturé his daughter's hand
in marriage. The old lord replied that all he had belonged to the king. At that moment the king was
advised that a person desired to deliver to him a message; and on going without, and conversing with Peter
Carlson, the Bishop of Calmar, he was seen to return
with high excitement and so much rapidity that his
guards could not keep pace with him, to the castle.
The news had just arrived that Duke John had escaped
from prison, and that the revolt had begun. Whether
the conveyance of this news to the king was timed at
this crisis by Persson in order to renew the king's hate
and terror of the imprisoned lords cannot be known;

but it is of a piece with all Persson's infernal management of the king; and the effect which Persson desired
was produced. The infuriated king rushed with drawn
dagger to the castle and entered the cell of Nils Sturé.
Lejonhufwud's room was next to that of Nils Sturé and
divided by so thin a partition that all that was done or
said in one room was heard in the other. Lejonhufwud
(who was saved) afterwards related that shortly before
the king's arrival Nils had sung a psalm, and had then
thrown himself on his bed and read aloud from his
Prayer Book. While he was thus lying, the king entered the cell with a drawn dagger in his hand, exclaiming, "Art thou still here, thou traitor?" Herr
Nils sprang from his bed, threw himself on his knees,
and said, "Most gracious king, I am not a traitor; but
I have faithfully served and risked my life for your majesty!" But the king answered him by striking him
with his dagger through the arm. Nils drew it out,
wiped off the blood, kissed the handle, and returned it
to the king, saying, "Good my lord, spare me; I have
not deserved displeasure." The king cried, "Hear how
that villain can supplicate for himself." One of the
king's guards, seeing what was the desire of the king,
completed the murder by seven wounds through his
body.

But no sooner was this done than Eric was seized
with remorse or the terror which in such a heart apes
remorse. He rushed to Swante Sturé's prison and threw
himself on his knees, and said: "Dear friend, for God's
sake be pleased to forgive us the evil which we have
done towards you"! The old lord wept bitterly, and
said: "Most gracious king, if my son has not suffered
damage to his life, I will forgive your majesty with all
my heart; but if his blood has been shed you must

answer to me for it before God."   "Ah," said Eric leap-
ing up, "you will never forgive us; therefore you shall
share their fate."   Thereupon he rushed out, ordered
the watch to have especial care of the prisoners, and
hurried out of the castle followed only by a few of his
guard.   He was beside himself, and no longer appeared
to know what he was doing.

Persson and his party now felt that the murder of
Nils Sturé would convince the king that no other course
remained but the execution of the imprisoned nobles.
But this design was opposed by Buerreus, the old tutor
of the king.   Horrified at the bloody purpose of Persson, and hoping that he might exert some influence
with a pupil who had continued to show him favor
and regard, he hastened out into the country to seek
the king.   He found him wandering wildly in a field,
and begged him to remember his royal dignity and
return to the castle.   Eric refused.   Buerreus also on his
knees implored him that he would not in haste order
the nobles in the castle to be killed.   Instead of an
answer Eric struck at him with a sword; but Buerreus
avoided the blow.   "Lame that rogue for me," cried
Eric to his guard.   Buerreus then turned and fled for
his life; but the same guardsman that had dispatched
Nils Sturé, Per Williamjson, sprung after him, over-
took him, cut off a calf of his leg and dispatched him
with his halberd.   A fit fate for one of the evil advisers
of the pupil who had now become his murderer.   After
this murder the king sent an order to the castle, whether
or no prompted by others cannot be known, that all
the prisoners should be executed with the exception
of Herr Stenbock.   And then escaping from his guards
he went deeper into the woods and wildernesses, and
no one knew what had become of him.

When the order for the execution came the Provost could not tell which Lord Stenbock—for there were two of that name—was intended to be excepted by the king. He went to consult Persson, whom he found at a gambling table, and who told him carelessly, without pausing in his game, that he must judge for himself. The Provost, in his doubt, saved the life of both the lords; but Swante Sture, his second son Eric, his kinsmen Abraham Stenbock and Ivar Ivarson, were executed. Thus closes this chapter amid scenes of horror. A frantic king wandering in the woods, and four of the best and highest nobles in the land lying murdered in the court of his castle.

CHAPTER VIII.

KING ERIC'S MADNESS, IMPRISONMENT AND DEATH. —DUKE JOHN BECOMES KING OF SWEDEN, AND HIS SON SIGISMUND KING OF POLAND.

The Mad-ness of King Eric. TWO days elapsed before King Eric could be found. He was discovered at last in the parish of Odensala in peasant's clothes, and apparently quite out of his mind. When he was addressed as king he exclaimed, " Nils Sturé is administrator of Sweden"! He had not eaten or slept for several days and could not be persuaded to take any thing from the fear of poison, until his mistress, Karin Mänsdotter, prepared and administered it with her own hands. When he awoke after a brief sleep he was overwhelmed with remorse for his crime and terror for its consequences. Or rather it would be more correct to say, in view of his subsequent position, that his terror put on the seeming of remorse. In the confusion which ensued, and the breaking up of the Diet, the government was administered by the council. At this time Eric was unable to discharge his kingly duties, and volunteered abject confessions of his guilt—and a declaration of the innocence of the murdered lords. He also distributed great sums of money to their relatives, and presents to the members of his estates. The king himself called this afterwards the period of his infirmity.

How far his madness was real—whether it was assumed to serve as a screen for his guilt—or how much
method there was in his madness, if he were really
mad, it is impossible to say.   It seems certain from
his subsequent defiant mood, in which he vindicated
and gloried in this deed as a fine stroke of kingcraft,
that it left no wound in his conscience.   On the one
hand, it cannot be doubted that either by a taint in his
nature, or by giving himself constantly to violent excitement—to the indulgence of excessive passions of
mind and body—he often acted like a madman.   But,
on the other hand, he often exhibited, as is common
in all stages of insanity, a degree of cunning which
seemed to prove that it was only the moral nature that
was deranged, and that the intellect was rather sharp-
ened than blunted by the loss of the moral sense.   An
eye-witness who belonged to his train, whose testimony
is quoted by Geijer, says: " He would not renounce the
government, feigning as if he had not reason until he
could first appease the nearest kinsmen of the deceased
lords."

Liberation The story of Duke John's escape from prison
of Duke had no foundation.   It was no doubt invented
John. to counteract the king's sudden access of remorse in which he promised to liberate the Sturés and
besought their forgiveness.   But the friends of John
now availed themselves of his real or affected mood of
penitence to urge his liberation.   Eric was readily induced to give his consent.   The duke promised the
faithful allegiance of a subject to his king and pledged
himself to recognize the sons of Karin Mänsdotter, the
mistress whom the king was now about to marry, as the
heirs to the throne.   The 8th of October was appointed
for the meeting of the brothers.   John, with his wife and

family, came by water to Swartsjö; and Eric and his suite met them in the gateway. Eric threw himself on his knees before John calling him his lord and sovereign. John also knelt, replying that Eric was king; but himself a poor prisoner who implored his royal mercy. They continued thus upon their knees opposite to each other until their stepmother, Katrina Stenlvock, came up and begged them to rise and not make themselves ridiculous in the eyes of all present. The brothers obeyed and proceeded together to the castle. But there was awkwardness and constraint in their bearing towards each other. Eric especially seemed anxious and melancholy and maudlin, repeatedly imploring the duchess and his little nephew Sigismund to forgive him for their imprisonment, and in so doing he again fell upon his knees. The duchess raised him and sought by words and caresses to calm him—but quite in vain. He left the room in a state of high excitement. John wisely feared lest this real or feigned remorse might pass again into real or feigned fury, and thought it advisable to retire soon to Wentholm. The reconciliation was completed by correspondence, and in it Eric offered to resign the government to John. After this John resided chiefly at Arboga and Eric at Stockholm; and thus ended the year 1567. In his diary the king had written over this date these words: "The most unfortunate year for King Eric." But he was destined to pass many other years still more unfortunate.

Recovery and proceedings of King Eric. For some time after this reconciliation with Duke John the mind of Eric exhibited frequent confusion—feigned or real. He sometimes wrote and spoke as if he considered John as king and himself as a prisoner. But gradually he reached

the mental position he had occupied previous to his supposed discovery of the conspiracy of the Sturés. He now
announced his purpose to marry Karin Mänsdotter, and
to have her crowned, as she subsequently was, queen of
Sweden. The war with Denmark having been prosecuted languidly, and to the great loss of the reputation
of the Swedish armies, Eric determined to carry it on in
person. The method he pursued showed the essential
frivolity of his character, and his love of extravagance
and display. He was extremely devoted to all warlike
ceremonialism and was as rigid and thorough a martinet
in discipline and drill, as he was incompetent as a leader.
His mind was absorbed at this time in getting from the
capital a large supply of red-colored goose feathers,
and squirrel and fox tails, for the new uniforms which
he devised, as well as wines and spices and raisins and
all the luxuries of his life in the palace of Stockholm.
But with characteristic caprice he soon returned to
the capital and celebrated his marriage with Karin
Mänsdotter with great splendor. But so distasteful
was this proceeding to his subjects, that those who
were selected to be knighted on that occasion could with
difficulty be persuaded to accept the doubtful honor.
Persson, on whom the sentence of death had been pronounced in the Council Chamber of Stockholm, when
the king was in his mood of penitence, and to whom
had been brought home the charge of having directly
intervened for the execution of more than a hundred
and twenty citizens and nobles, but whom the king had
forgiven and restored to power, resumed his old influence, and was still the evil genius of the king and the
horror and bane of the kingdom. He persuaded the
king to demand from those on whom, in his hour of
madness, he had lavished excessive gifts, that they

should be returned. At the same time he put forth a proclamation in reference to the aberration of his mind and his proceedings under its influence in the preceding year, in which he made his servants responsible for the crimes which he had himself urged on against the remonstrances of at least one of his most honored counselors, Buerreus, who suffered the penalty of his rash advice by the brutal murder to which he was subjected by the order of the king. He alleged that in fear of an outbreak of revolt he had put to death Nicholas Sturé, who was rightly condemned for his proved treason; but his servants on that occasion, *against his own will*, had cut off the innocent as well as the guilty. He himself had fled to the wilds (and this aberration is represented as if it were the consequence of the guilt of his servants and not of his own), deserted by all, reckoning himself at last a deposed captive, and despairing in this condition, not only of his throne, but even of his eternal salvation. Meantime the government had been neglected and the kingdom ruined; but now God had restored him to his health and faculties, and the exercise of regal authority; and he therefore ordained an universal thanksgiving over the whole of Sweden. He had the effrontery to exhort the nobles to set to the people the example of an honorable and useful life; for, said this human devil turned preacher, " Ye were not raised to the class of nobles in intent and act merely that ye should lead merry days and do no good in return to the realm of Sweden."

Events which led to a Revolt. The fatal events of the previous year, and the marriage of the king to a mistress of the class of peasants, could not fail to produce profound discontent throughout the kingdom. But other events occurred and were made known, which rendered it quite impossible that so depraved and vile a monarch could long remain upon the throne in a nation that retained the least of that spirit of independence and self-assertion which had been exhibited even in exaggerated forms in the earlier portion of the reign of the great Gustavus.

1. *Ivan the Terrible of Russia.* It was certainly a most disastrous circumstance for nothern and eastern Europe that two such monarchs as Eric and Ivan the Terrible of Russia should have reigned contemporaneously. There was no little resemblance between these two crowned monsters. They were both subject to fits of frenzy. Those of Ivan were more awful in their results than those of Eric, because they were longer in their duration, and because his power was more absolute and the reach of his tyranny more extensive, and because his wildest and most cruel decrees were implicitly carried into execution. It is not essential to the events which I am about to describe, in which Ivan and Eric were concerned, that I should present this companion picture of another mad tyrant, whose atrocities seem colossal by the side of those of the king of Sweden; but the description will better enable us to realize the horrors of that wild time, and to appreciate the guilt of Eric in entering into a nefarious compact with one whose frantic crimes it would seem might have appalled even him. I quote from Kelly's Compendium of Karamsin, a native Russian author.

"In his first fit of rage several great boyars of the family of Ruric (the old royal line) were put to death by beheading, poisoning, or impaling; their wives and children were driven naked into the forests, where they expired under the scourge. In a second paroxysm he marched as a conqueror against the subjugated Novo-

gorod; and imagining that he imitated or perhaps surpassed the victory of his grandfather, he butchered
with his own hand a throng of the unfortunate inhabitants whom he had heaped together in a vast inclosure,
and when at last his strength failed to second his fury,
he gave up the remainder to his select guards, to his
slaves, to his dogs, and to the opened ice of the Bolkof
in which, for more than a month, these hapless beings
were daily ingulfed by hundreds. Then declaring
that his justice was satisfied he retired; seriously re-
commending him to the prayers of the survivors; who
took especial care not to neglect the orders of their
terrestrial deity.

"Tver and Pskof also experienced his presence; Moscow at length saw him again and on the same day the
public square was covered with red-hot brasiers, enormous cauldrons of brass, and eighty gibbets. Five
hundred of the most illustrious nobles, already torn by
tortures, were dragged thither; some were massacred
amid the joyful acclamations of his savage satellites;
but the major part expired under the protracted agony
of being slashed with knives by the courtiers of the
Muscovite monster.

"Nor were women spared any more than men; Ivan
ordered them to be hanged at their own doors; and he
prohibited their husbands from going out and in without passing under the corpses of their companions till
they rotted and dropped to pieces on them. Elsewhere
husbands or children were fastened dead at the places
which they had occupied at the domestic table, and
their wives or mothers were compelled to sit opposite
to their dear and lifeless remains.

"To the dogs and bears which this raging madman
delighted to let loose upon the people, was left the

task of clearing the public square from the mutilated bodies which encumbered it. According to the annals of Pskof there were 60,000 victims at Novogorod alone. Every day Ivan invented new modes of punishment which his tyrrany, jaded by so many excesses, still looked upon as insufficient. Very soon he required fratricides and parricides! Basmanof was compelled to kill his father; Prozoroosky his brother. The monster next drowned eight hundred women; and rummaging with atrocious cupidity the abodes of his victims he, by dint of shocking tortures, compelled the remaining relations to point out the places in which their wealth was hidden. These confiscations, joined to monopolies, taxes and conquests, accumulated in his palace the riches of the empire and the Tartars.

"Setting himself above all laws this lustful being married seven wives. Even his daughter-in-law was forced to fly from his death-bed, terrified by his lasciviousness. He was eager to procure an eighth wife from the court of his friend Elizabeth of England; and the daughter of the earl of Huntington was offered to the inspection of the Russian embassador, at her own desire and the queen's. The daughter of Henry VIII. was not shocked to hear, at the same time, of the czar's wish to be married, and of the birth of a prince born to him by his seventh living wife; but before the English match was concluded Mary Hastings took fright, and begged Elizabeth to spare her the perilous honor. To complete Ivan's usurpation he assumed the manner of one who was inspired; and by all those external signs which our bounded imagination attribute to the Divinity, he made himself God in the minds of his people. All that came from his hands, blows, wounds, even the most degrading treatment, was received with resignation, nay adoration. In the blind and servile submission of the Russian people God and czar were identified; their proverbial sayings bear witness to this. This was the national formula of speech in reference to anything future: 'If God and the czar wills it.' If there is in history the record of a more horrible royal monster, and of one who exercised such atrocious and wanton and widespread cruelty and desolation among his own subjects, I know not where to find it."

2. *Relation of Eric to Ivan.* When the proposal of Duke John for the hand of the Polish princess, Catherine, was made, it was found that Ivan was also her suitor. But the czar and Sigismund not being able to agree upon the terms of the marriage contract, the suit of the czar was rejected. The Poles, who had been at war with the Russians for hundreds of years, intensely hated them; and to show their contempt for Ivan sent him instead of Catherine a female figure, a large doll, in a splendid wedding dress. The czar was furious, and invaded and cruelly ravaged Poland. But this did not satisfy him. He was determined to get possession of Catherine, notwithstanding her marriage to Duke John.

When King Eric was married to Karin Mänsdotter, John and his brothers returned thanks for the invitation to the wedding; but did not dare to go. Duke John had learned that Eric had secretly promised in 1556 to deliver his wife into the hands of Ivan, on condition that the czar would desist from his claims on Eastland and assist him against the Poles. It is a striking evidence of the degradation to which the tyranny of Eric had brought his subservient officials that the eminent chancellor Nicholas Gillenstierna, in February, 1567, actually subscribed at Moscow a convention by which

Eric engaged to give up his sister-in-law to the czar on the conditions named above. After John and his wife were liberated it was no longer in Eric's power to fulfill this promise. But a Russian embassy to Stockholm demanded its fulfillment, and a letter from Eric to Ivan, in April, 1568, shows that the negotiations were not yet ended. These facts coming to the knowledge of John seemed to absolve him from all further loyalty to his brother. The marriage of Eric and the growing weariness and detestation of the people for his cruel and capricious rule gave the opportunity, and the last contemplated outrage upon himself and wife furnished the motive and vindication of his rebellion.

Rebellion of the Dukes. Only four days after Eric's wedding he learned of the revolt of the brothers, John and Charles. They took possession of Wadstena on the Lake Wetter, a central and populous part of the country; and were soon joined by many adherents. The brothers met for their first conference on this matter under an oak in Wormland; and when they gathered their followers at · Wadstena, oak-leaves in their hats and caps were adopted to commemorate the event, and to designate their party. The proclamation which they issued must have been convincing and acceptable to the realm. The principal charges made against Eric were—"that he had often violated his faith to God and man; that he had kept his brother Duke John, with his wife and children, five years in prison, without having been convicted of any crime; that he had murdered several innocent lords at Upsala; that he had designed to assassinate several others, together with his two brothers, at his marriage; that to the great scandal of the royal family, he had made his concubine, a person of peasant origin, queen of Sweden. To this they added that he would have given up the Duke John's wife to Ivan of Russia; that contrary to his pledges he had restored the infamous Persson to place, and his old influence; and, in fine, that he had committed many vile and infamous actions unworthy the majesty of a king " (Puffendorf, 246). I pass over the rapid successive steps which ended in the capture of Eric in the early part of 1569. Brought to trial he conducted his own defense. When at one point Duke John interrupted him with the exclamation that he was out of his senses, he answered: " Once only was I out of my senses—when I let thee slip from prison." His condemnation and imprisonment were foregone conclusions. His harsh treatment was not honorable to John, whose imprisonment had been made so light by Eric. Several unsuccessful plots for his release were made. These were so numerous and alarming that Duke John gave directions that in certain emergencies he should be poisoned. This took place the 25th of February, 1577, in the forty-ninth year of his age, and the ninth of his imprisonment. It was the fit end of an awful life.

State of Religion during this Reign. Very little that can properly be called Church History is to be found during the wild and troubled reign of Eric. When he was, as he supposed, about to proceed to England for the hand of Queen Elizabeth, he put forth a decree to abolish some of the ceremonies of the Lutheran Church, and to bring it into nearer conformity to the doctrine and discipline of the Reformed. This was done under the influence of his former tutor, Buerreus, a Frenchman, and under the impression probably that such a proceeding would commend him and the proposed match to the favorable regard of Elizabeth. But the archbishop and the people were too devoted to the Lutheran

system to be at all influenced by this decree. It remained wholly inoperative.

At the same time a Nuncio from the Pope, John
Francis, came to Sweden in order to bring back the
king and the country to the Papal obedience. The
name of the Nuncio suggests his probable English origin and the connection of the embassy with the design
of securing the return of Queen Elizabeth to the Papal
obedience, and of influencing her in that direction by
gaining over Eric, who it was generally believed was
an accepted suitor of the queen. That this secret
Nuncio labored to pave the way for that Catholic
reaction which was subsequently attempted by King
John is a matter of course. But the kingdom had been
brought by Gustavus into such a firm hold upon Lutheranism, consecrated in the memory of the people
by all the glorious struggles and triumphs of his now
lamented reign, that neither the Reformed nor the
Roman Church could make any progress in the way of
winning proselytes.

Duke John proclaimed King. The two dukes had labored in concert for
the overthrow of Eric. During the progress
of the revolt, an equal homage and acknowledgment of obedience, on the part of the people, was
rendered to both brothers. It was at first arranged
that they were to reign together. There is evidence
that such was originally declared to be the arrangement agreed upon by the brothers, and assented to by
their partisans. Puffendorf declares that it was confirmed by an oath on the part of John; and that the first
money that was coined bore the names and effigies of
both the princes. But this arrangement was manifestly
impracticable. Yet it was well for the success of
their enterprise that such should be, or should be be-

lieved to be, the design, in order that there might be
unity of counsel and of action. When the brothers
succeeded in their enterprise the seniority of John
and his government of Stockholm were immediately
and treacherously taken advantage of by him to secure the acknowledgment of him as king. The Council accepted him as such on his arrival, and the
Estates confirmed the recognition. Charles did not
disguise his dissatisfaction, and could not, or did
not drop the tone of an equal in all his transac-
tions with his brother. Endowed with far more force
of mind and power of will than John, he did not fail to
exercise a controlling voice in the government, and
to dominate over his less gifted and energetic brother.
He was the only one of the sons of Gustavus who inherited his father's great intellectual and administrative
capacity, his decision of character, and his thoroughly
conscientious and pronounced Protestantism. But
while in these respects he resembled his father, he was
wanting in that geniality and friendliness, and charm
of manner and adaptation to all classes which won for
Gustavus such enthusiastic affection and regard. But
while Charles represented his father in his higher characteristics, his weaker brother represented him in his
more popular traits; and was thus enabled to hold his
place upon the throne notwithstanding proceedings
on his part which were repugnant to the national
will and conscience.

Privileges bestowed up-on the No-bility. The first care of King John was to strengthen
himself by renewing the old privileges of the
nobility and bestowing upon them new immunities. He reversed the attainder pronounced upon the great families whose chiefs were
destroyed by Eric. He restored to the nobles the

right of collecting the taxes due from their dependents to the king. The supreme court established by Eric, whose effect was to centralize the powers of the kingdom in the government at Stockholm, and to limit the independence of the lords, was abolished. Accused nobles were not to be incarcerated until after conviction. The policy of Gustavus was to increase the powers and resources of the nobility in order that, bound to the king by benefits received and hoped for, they might add both strength and *éclat* to the throne. The effect of the policy of John, which it cost King Charles many efforts and long years to undo, was to add to the prerogatives of the nobles; and at the same time to weaken the ties which bound them to the throne.

Sigismund elected King of Poland. The election of Sigismund, son of King John, to the throne of Poland is the event which, fostered by the vascillating policy and the uncertain position of his father, led to the counter-Reformation. It will be necessary to refer to some of the circumstances which preceded this event.

1. *The Condition of Poland.* Poland was unlike, in many respects, any other kingdom in Europe. Its development was not, like that of Germany and France, from a feudal system, in which a limited number of great lords towered high above all the other classes of the population. During the Jagallon dynasty, 1384 to 1572, which reigned nearly two centuries, the throne had been hereditary, but its power had been extremely limited by their diets. These diets were in theory, and at first largely in fact, composed of the army, which consisted of only those called nobles. There were but two classes of the Polish population, the nobles who composed the army, and the serfs and agricultural laborers. The

trading and mechanic classes consisted chiefly of Jews,
and the professions were filled by Germans. Of these
nobles some few were large proprietors; but the greater
number were poor, and could not break through the
traditions which their nobility imposed upon them, and
enter, in the intervals of warfare, into lucrative professions. It was a state of society, a form of polity, quite
unique—one which of necessity led to many wars, and
was not calculated to promote domestic quiet.

2. *The Diets.* Up to the beginning of the fifteenth
century the diets had been general assemblies of all the
nobles;—that is, in fact, of the army. But the growing
inconvenience of holding meetings of more than 100,000
horsemen on an open plain, and of securing intelligible
and well considered laws and regulations from such an
assembly, obliged the Poles at length to adopt a system
of representation. Minor diets or *colloquia* had long
been held by each of the Palatines in their palatinates
for the administration of justice, and these now began
ʻto appoint deputies to the national diet. In the course
of time each of these districts adopted this system;
and about 1468 the custom had become nearly universal
of sending from each palatinate two deputies to the
general diet. The development of this system was
very gradual, and it was never universally adopted.
Some of the old nobles, tenacious of their traditional
rights, refused to transfer them to a deputy. The deputies were bound to act precisely according to the
directions of their constituents. At this period also
the towns secured the elective franchise; and were permitted to send deputies to the diet of the palatinate,
and all of them in combination, within one of these
districts, could also send their two deputies to the
general diet. It was a singular system. An heredi-

tary monarchy of very limited powers, controlled by an army calling itself a nobility, which was at the same time the only national legislature; and at this period both the king and nobility, for the maintenance or increase of their prerogatives, seeking the aid of the new power, the representatives of the towns and cities. The only prerogative which gave power and dignity to the crown was that of appointment to all offices in the kingdom.

3. *Literary Culture of the Nobility.* Though a large portion of the nobility were poor, they were, as a class, unusually cultivated and learned. Their enforced exclusion from all professions, except that of war, drove large numbers of them into the pursuit and enjoyment of learning. The Latin language was very generally understood, and, as spoken and written, was almost as widely used among the better classes of Germans and Jews, as well as among the Poles, as the vernacular. When, after the death of the last king of the hereditary dynasty of Jagallon, 1572, the monarchy became elective, Henry, Duke of Anjou, son of Catherine de Medici, and brother of Charles IX., was elected king. An embassy was sent to Paris to announce the decision; and the description given of this Polish deputation, by an eye witness of its reception, confirms the statement which I have made of the relative superiority in culture of the Poles, at this period, to persons of the same class in other countries. The account is taken from the great French historian, De Thou.

"It is impossible to express the general astonishment when we saw these embassadors in long robes, fur caps, sabres, arrows and quivers; but our admiration was excessive when we saw the sumptuousness

of their equipages, the scabbards of their swords
adorned with jewels, their bridles, saddles, and horse
cloths decked in the same way, and the air of consequence and dignity by which they were distinguished.
One of the most remarkable circumstances was their
facility in expressing themselves in Latin, French,
German, and Italian. These four languages were as
familiar to them as their vernacular tongue. There
were only two men in court who could answer them
in Latin, the Baron of Millau and the Marquis of
Castlenau. They had been commissioned expressly
to support the honor of the French nation; but they
had reason to blush at their comparative ignorance
in this point. The embassadors spoke our language
with so much purity, that one would have taken them
rather for men educated upon the banks of the Seine,
than for the inhabitants of the countries which were
watered by the Vistula and the Dnieper, which put
our courtiers to the blush, who knew nothing, but
were open enemies of all science; so that when their
guests questioned them they answered only with signs
or blushes."

4. *Religious Toleration in Poland.* It is another
remarkable characteristic of the condition of Poland
that under the Jagallon dynasty, while Catholicism
was the religion of the state, a free toleration to all
other systems was allowed. It is a striking spectacle
in the midst of the stormy and intolerant sixteenth
century, when the Papacy and the Reformation everywhere else studied to exclude each other:—that of
full and free toleration and kindly feeling, among all
churches and all forms of faith. I quote a description
of this state of things from Fletcher's "History of
Poland."

"There were perhaps more printing-presses at this time—*i. e.,* in the sixteenth century—in Poland than there have ever been since, or than there were in any other country of Europe at the time. There were eighty-three towns where they printed books; and in Cracow alone there were fifty presses. The chief circumstances which supported so many printing-houses in Poland at this time was the liberty of the press; which allowed the publication of the writings of all the contending sects, which were not permitted to be printed elsewhere.

"Nor were the Poles less advanced in that most enlightened feeling of civilization,—religious toleration. When almost all the rest of Europe was deluged with the blood of contending sectaries; while the Lutherans were perishing in Germany; while the blood of a hundred thousand Protestants, the victims of the war of persecution, and the horrid massacre of St. Bartholomew, was crying from the ground of France against the infamous Triumvirate and the hypocritical Catherine de Medici; while Mary made England a fiery ordeal of persecution; and even the heart of the virgin queen was not entirely cleansed of the foul stuff of bigotry, but dictated the burning of the Arians—Poland opened an asylum for all religions and allowed every man to worship God in his own way. 'Mosques,' says Rulhiere, ' were raised among churches and synagogues. Leopol has always been the seat of three bishops, Greek, Armenian and Latin; and it was never inquired which of the three cathedrals any man who consented to submit to the regulations of government went to receive the communion. Lastly, when the Reformation was rending so many states into inimical factions, Poland, without proscribing her ancient

religion, received into her bosom the two new sects.'
All parties were allowed a perfect liberty of the
press. The Catholics printed their books at Cracow,
Posen, Lubin, etc., while the followers of the Confes-
sion of Augsburg published theirs in Paniowicka,
Dombrow, etc.; the Reformers at Pinczow, Brzese,
Neiswiez; the Arians in Racow and Baslaw; and the
Greek sectarians in Lithuania, at Ostrow and Wilna."

Such was the state of the kingdom when Sigismund
II., the last of the kings of the house of Jagallon, died
in 1572.

5. *Catholic Reaction in Poland.* On the death of
Sigismund II., and the extinction of the Jagallon
dynasty, Poland seemed about to be delivered up
to hopeless anarchy. The crown was formally made
over to his subjects by the dying king. Poland became henceforward an elective monarchy. After a
decorous interval, in which the kingdom was administered by the council of state, the archbishop, Gnesne,
convoked a diet for considering the steps proper to
be taken for the election of a new king. The partisans
and lovers of the old method of assembling all the
nobles at the national diets prevailed in securing the
decision that all the nobles should have a voice in
the election of the king. It was resolved that all the
nobles of the kingdom should meet in a large plain
near Warsaw. Such a spectacle was never elsewhere
seen—thousands of nobles on horseback, in military
costume, assembled to elect a king. In this so-called
diet the coronation oath, or *pacta conventa*, was re-
vised. Its provisions remained unaltered until the
dismemberment of Poland by Prussia and Russia. It
stripped the monarch of all power except that of executing the laws framed by the diet, with the single,

but important, exception of appointments to all the offices in the kingdom. It made the crown elective and provided for the regular convocation of the diet every two years. It bound the king and the kingdom to perfect toleration of all religions. The Roman Catholic however remained the state religion, and the kings were bound to be of that profession of faith.

The nobles accordingly assembled on the plain near Warsaw; and most picturesque and brilliant, and certainly unique, was the scene and the proceedings. Several candidates were nominated, among whom were King John of Sweden; Ernest, son of the emperor Maximilian of Austria; and Henry, Duke of Anjou, son of Catherine de Medici and brother of Charles IX., then king of France. The latter was elected; that is, he was accepted, not by a counted and ascertained majority, but by a louder acclaim and clash of arms than greeted the announcement of any other name. No sooner however had he reluctantly reached Poland, than he was informed of the death of Charles, which left him the rightful heir of the throne of France. Knowing that the Poles would not allow him to violate the oath which bound him to reside in Poland, he resolved to leave, and did leave, the kingdom by stealth. He was overtaken a few leagues from Cracow by a Polish nobleman, but resolutely refused to return.

The next person elected was Stephen Batory, Duke of Transylvania, the husband of Anne, the sister of the late king Sigismund. He was a prince of rare virtues and eminent talent. In his wars with Russia he gained great renown, no less for his signal victories, than for the contrast of his just and elevated spirit with the barbarous and vindictive character of his Russian foes.

It was under this wise and just king that the Romanists acquired a great increase of influence and power. They did not succeed in changing the laws which enforced toleration, but they put themselves, through the mistaken policy of the king, at the sources of religious influence, which greatly extended the power of the Papacy and threatened to bring the kingdom again into absolute obedience to the Pope. The peace between Poland and Russia was brought about through the agency of Possevin, the Jesuit, and Legate of the Pope. This led to the introduction of the Jesuits into Poland. That order was of high reputation for its learning; and the king, ignorant of their history and principles, imagined that he was promoting the welfare of his kingdom when he intrusted to them the care of the University of Wilna, which he had just founded. But there, as everywhere in Europe, they soon showed themselves in a different character from that of peaceful teachers, which it was their policy, when they wished to get possession of a kingdom, to assume.

The successive steps by which this influence was acquired are stated by Ranke with his usual clearness:

"An opinion has been expressed that the Protestants, who for a time certainly had as we have seen the decided supremacy in Poland, would also have been in a condition to raise a king of their own faith to the throne, but that even they themselves came at length to consider a Catholic more advantageous, because in the person of the Pope he had still a higher power and judge placed over him.

"If this were so they brought a very heavy punishment upon themselves for a decision so adverse to Protestantism.

"For it was precisely by the agency of a Catholic king that the Pope was able to make war on them.

"Of all the foreign embassadors to Poland the Papal Nuncios alone possessed the right of demanding audience of the king without the presence of a senator. We know what these men were. They had prudence and address enough to cultivate and profit by the confidential intercourse thus placed within their reach.

"In the beginning of the eightieth year of the sixteenth century Cardinal Bolognetto was the Nuncio in Poland. He complained of the severity of the climate; of the cold to which as an Italian he was doubly susceptible; of the close, suffocating air in the small heated rooms; and of the whole mode of life which was utterly uncongenial to his habits and predilections. He nevertheless accompanied King Stephen from Warsaw to Cracow, from Wilna to Lubin—throughout the kingdom in short; at times in rather a melancholy mood, but none the less indefatigable. During the campaign he kept up his intercourse with the king at least by letter and maintained an uninterrupted connection between the interests of Rome and the royal personage.

"We have a circumstantial relation of his official proceedings and from this we learn the character of his undertakings and how far he prospered in them.

"Above all things he exhorted the king to appoint only Catholics to government offices; to permit no other worship than that of the Catholic Church in the royal towns; and to re-establish the tithes—measures which were adopted about the same time in other countries and which promoted or indicated the renovation of Catholicism.

"But the Nuncio was not wholly successful in the first instance. King Stephen thought he could not go

so far; he declared that he was not sufficiently powerful to venture it.   Yet this prince was not only imbued
with Catholic convictions he had besides an innate
zeal for the interests of the Church, and in many particulars his decisions were regulated by the representations of the Nuncio.

"It was under the immediate patronage of royalty
that the Jesuit colleges in Cracow, Gradno, and
Puttusk were established.   The new calendar was
introduced without difficulty and the ordinances of
the Council of Trent were for the most part carried
into full effect.   But the most important circumstance was the king's determination that the bishoprics should for the future be bestowed on Catholics
only.   Protestants had previously made their way even
to these ecclesiastical dignities; but the Nuncio was
now authorized to summon them before his tribunal
and to depose them; a fact of all the more importance
inasmuch as that a seat and vote in the senate were
attached to the episcopal office.   It was this political
efficacy of the spiritual institutions that the Nuncio
most especially sought to turn to account.   Above all
he exhorted the bishops to be unanimous as regarded
the measures to be adopted at the Diet, and these
measures were prescribed by himself.   With the most
powerful of the Polish ecclesiastics, the Archbishop
Gnesne, the Archbishop of Cracow, Bolognetto had
formed a close personal intimacy which was of infinite
utility for the promotion of his views.   Thus he succeeded not only in awakening new zeal among the
clergy, but also in at once obtaining extensive influence over temporal affairs.   The English were making
proposals for a commercial treaty with Poland which
promised to be very advantageous, more particularly

for Dantzic. It was by the Nuncio alone that this purpose was defeated, and principally because the English required a distinct promise that they should be allowed to trade and live in peace without being persecuted on account of their religion.

"These things suffice to show that, however moderate King Stephen might be, it was yet under him that Catholicism acquired an essential reinstation in Poland."

It was under these circumstances that Sigismund III., son of King John of Sweden, was elected King of Poland. His mother, Catherine Jagellonica, had borne him in prison, and so carefully trained him in the Catholic faith that he remained immovably fixed in it, notwithstanding that his boyhood and youth were passed in the midst of the Lutheranism of Sweden.

CHAPTER IX

IN the last chapter, after a description of the events which resulted in the accession of Duke John to the throne of Sweden, and an account of his general political policy in the administration of the kingdom, there followed a sketch of the condition of Poland up to the period of the election of Sigismund, the son of King John, to the throne of that country. It may seem that it would have been a more natural course to have proceeded with the narrative of events in Sweden up to the period of the election of Sigismund; and *then* to have given that sketch of the affairs of Poland to the time when they became implicated with those of Sweden. It seemed, however, that in proceeding with the story of John's reign, a more definite impression of it would be conveyed if the narrative were not interrupted by a description of the condition of Poland previous to the election of Sigismund; and if we were so far in possession of its history as to follow intelligently the proceedings in which the two kingdoms were subsequently involved.

Political Condition from 1568 to 1583. During the whole period in which those ecclesiastical events occurred King John was constantly engaged in war with Denmark or with Russia. The war with Denmark he had inherited on his accession, 1568, from Eric. A disgraceful truce for six months, to be consummated by a more disgraceful peace, which had been entered into by Eric, was disavowed by the States under King John. War was resumed to the advantage of Sweden; and the Congress of Stettin, under the mediation of the Emperor of Austria, the King of France, and the Elector of Saxony, concluded a peace in 1570 which was advantageous and honorable to Sweden. But the war with Russia, in which the possession of Livonia was contested, and which led to successful Swedish invasions and great victories in Russia, and to horrible barbarities on the part of Ivan the Terrible in Finland, was not closed until 1582.

First Measure for Restoration of Romanism. Immediately after his coronation at Upsala King John confirmed his brother Charles in the government of Sudermania, Nericia and Wormland, which had been assigned to him in the last will of Gustavus. This he did, not only to give him some satisfaction for depriving him of an equal position in the government of the kingdom, but also to remove him from Stockholm, that he might not be able to counteract the measures which the king had determined upon for the restoration of Romanism. His policy was not to attempt at once and violently to restore it; but gradually to prepare the way for its introduction, by so modifying the liturgy and increasing the splendor of the ceremonies, as to create a taste and habit which would not ultimately be satisfied with anything less than the full restoration of the Romish system. Soon after his coronation he proposed to the clergy some articles relating to the vestments to be used in the public worship and the garments to be ordinarily worn by the clergy, which would present them to the people in a garb closely resembling that of the

Romish ecclesiastics. Other regulations concerning discipline and dependence upon the bishops were proposed which had the same design. But these articles were at once rejected by the clergy. The movement of the king was premature, abrupt and unskillful. It produced just that conviction of his intention to restore Romanism which he wished to disguise.

Abp. Nericius' Summary of Luther- an Doctrine. After concluding a peace with Denmark, 1570, King John again, and in a more skillful manner, resumed his settled purpose to bring back the kingdom to obedience to the Pope. Having heard that the Archbishop Nericius, of Stockholm, had composed a work which was intended as a summary of the Christian doctrine as held by the Swedish Church, he requested the archbishop to allow him to see it before it should be published. Having read it over he persuaded the archbishop to leave out some of the most pronounced statements of the Lutheran doctrine; and to state some points in controversy between the Lutheran and Catholic Church in vague and general phraseology. The archbishop not only consented to these modifications but also to the statement at the close of the book, "that there were several things wanting to render it complete, which he recommended his successor to supply." The king also succeeded in having it sanctioned by synodical authority; which gave it the same position in the Swedish Church as the Apology of Jewel and that of Melancthon occupied in the Churches of England and Germany. But the book was not allowed to pass unquestioned. Some of the clergy exposed its unsound or unsatisfactory statements; but, as usual in such cases, a party arose in the kingdom favorable, not as yet to the reinstatement of the Papal power, but to an advanced doctrinal system, approaching that of Rome, and to the introduction of a higher and more showy ritual. The device of the king seemed, as a first step, to be successful.

Policy of the King. So strongly, however, did the majority of the clergy adhere to the Augsburg Confession, that the king found it necessary to declare that his design was the same as that of some of the Lutheran divines in Germany, who labored to bring Romanists and Lutherans to unite upon the basis of the doctrine and discipline of the undivided Church of the first six centuries. Such had been the policy of Ferdinand I. of Austria in his later days—a policy which he attempted to accomplish through the agency of Cassander, a Lutheran divine, and of two of his Roman theologians, Staphylus and Wizel. This, however, was not the real object of the king. The avowed design of Cassander was his real one; whereas King John hypocritically professed to adopt it only with the view to pass onward from it to full union with the Church of Rome. This scheme had proved to be quite impracticable in Germany, as John well knew; but it might serve to deceive those who were alarmed at the innovations which seemed to look Romeward. "And to compass his design the better," says Puffendorf, "he called a convocation of the bishops and ministers of every diocese at Stockholm, to consult about the choice of a new archbishop; to whom he represented how many heresies daily grew up in Europe; and how great troubles and disorders they had occasioned in the Low Countries, France and Germany; whence he inferred that it was best to adhere to the doctrine of the Catholic and Apostolic Church. To which he added, that when their predecessors had gone about to destroy the ancient errors they had also at the same time abolished several good and decent ordinances, to the great prejudice of piety."

A new Liturgy. The king gradually induced his clergy to accept a Liturgy which was, in large part, his own work, and which was a near approach to the offices of the Roman Church. The service for the administration of the eucharist, which was called a mass, and bore a great resemblance to the Roman office, was the first changed form that was accepted by the clergy. John made its acceptance the condition of filling the long vacant sees of Linkoping and of Westeras. But, even after their election, the king would not consent to confirm them in their temporalities until they had signed some Articles in which they pledged their consent to further alterations in the Liturgy. The king then summoned a synod at Stockholm for the revision of all the forms and offices of the Church, with the professed view of bringing them into conformity with those of the Church of the first six centuries. Under the pressure of the king and of the newly consecrated bishops the synod consented to the proposed changes. They introduced several ceremonies of the Romish Church, such especially as related to the sacraments and the consecration of priests and bishops. This formulary was called "*The Liturgy of the Church of Sweden, according to the Catholic and Orthodox Church*," and was published in Latin and Swedish, that at first they might make use of both languages; and that when the people should become accustomed to it they might drop the use of the Swedish altogether.

Agency of the Pope in these Movements. It is not to be supposed that the Pope would remain ignorant or an inactive spectator of these proceedings. The character of John was such as to lay him open to flatteries and intrigues

of subtle Papists and to the influence of his noble and
gifted wife. He was a man of large learning,—speak-
ing and writing readily and well German, French, Italian, and English; and able to make long Latin speeches
without premeditation. Theology was the science of
the age and during his long imprisonment he devoted
himself to it; and at first seemed really to have adopted
the views of Cassander, which he subsequently brought
forward as a blind to his purpose of introducing Romanism. But, says Geijer, "We should do him too
much honor if we should suppose that he had penetrated to the core of the question. He loved hie-
rarchic like all other pomp, and devised ceremonies
for divine worship, as he did arms for the provinces,
decorations for his buildings, and additions to his
titles."

On such a nature it was easy for the Pope to work.
The queen's zeal was stimulated by the praises which
she received from Rome. Cardinal Stanislaus Hosius
wrote to her that she was extolled to heaven on account of her care for the eternal salvation of her husband. "He had already," the letter continued, "intimated his wish that some learned and pious Jesuits
should be sent to him. Hereof the whole city con-
verses." In another letter the cardinal reproaches her
"for suffering herself to be persuaded by the king to
take the Holy Supper under both forms of bread and
wine, instructing her how to answer the objections of
her husband, and at the same time bring him back
gradually to the bosom of the Church. She must exhort him first to restore priests to office, and to resume
the celebration of the mass. If that were done, then
the Church, as a tender-mother, might even permit the
use of the cup to the laity. This was written in 1572.

Two years later the same promise is repeated, with the
condition, however, that some token of return to the use
of the mass must be given before negotiations can be
opened for the restoration of the cup. In a letter to
the king in 1576 the cardinal expresses his gratification
that the return to the ceremonies was being gradually
effected; and in another letter, of October, 1577, he
thanks God for the king's conversion. When the two
Jesuits, Florentius Fayt and Laurentius Novegus, came
to Stockholm they gave themselves out as evangelical
preachers. From the labors of the latter the cardinal
expected great results, because as a Norwegian he
could make himself easily understood by the people.
" Seek above all," he wrote to John Herbst, the queen's
court chaplain, " that he may obtain a church wherein
to preach. Let him avoid offense. Let him extol
faith to heaven, and depreciate works without faith,
preaching Christ as the only Mediator and His cross as
the only means of salvation; thereupon let him show
that nothing else has been preached in the Papacy."
That Rome regarded all measures against Protestants
as lawful, appears not only from this incident, but from
another which occurred just previous to the same period. When Henry of Valois, in 1573, was elected king
of Poland, the cardinal advises that the Protestants
there abiding should be fed with hopes until after the
coronation; but if the king had even promised them on
oath, the freedom of their religion, he was not bound
to its observance.

Condition of the Church on Accession of King John. The deplorable condition into which the
church had fallen during the reign of Eric,
greatly favored the designs of John. He
made it to appear that he was laboring for
a restoration, rather than for the overthrow, of the old

church order. In the Articles concerning the clergy, issued in 1569 and 1574, complaints are made that ignorant students were called to the priesthood; that homicides, topers, and adulterers, exercised it with impunity; that many clergymen neglected their calling for trade and other secular business; that they gave no thought to their sermon, before they came into the church, and then read out of the Book of Homilies what came to hand, whether or not it might suit the gospel of the day; that they went to the altar in torn or unclean vestments, and dispensed the sacraments with foul hands. Many churches had fallen into decay and ruin. The church plate had disappeared so entirely that clay vessels were used in the dispensation of the sacraments, notwithstanding, as the king complained, the clergy had silver cups in their own houses. The nobility and possessors of the tithes held not only the crown's two-thirds of the tithes, but also often that portion of them which was intended for the maintenance of the church and clergy. The king issued repeated prohibitions against this abuse, and expended large sums on the erection and improvement of the churches, and on the provision of proper vessels and suitable decorations for the orderly and reverent administration of the ordinances of divine worship. He would even provide for the reclothing of ragged priests who came in his way. All these measures tended to reconcile the clergy and the people to his innovations in the public service, so long as they could regard them as evidences of his mere harmless eccentricity, or his high ritualistic tastes.

The Kirk's Ordinance of Abp. Laurentius Petri. The aged and faithful archbishop, a decided Protestant, endeavored to counteract the design of the king, and at the same time to reform the deplorable evils of the church. He drew up in 1571 the Kirk's Ordinance, which was sanctioned by a synod. Some of its regulations were new, called out by the evils of the time, and others were a republication of regulations which had fallen into disuse or neglect. A new regulation, in the Protestant direction, provided that a call or an assent of the congregation should be obtained before a priest should be instituted. To the bishop was given the power of refusing ordination to candidates whom he judged to be incompetent or unworthy. The candidate for ordination was required to be at least "tolerably conversant with the Holy Scriptures." He was bound to understand the Latin language and to be able to speak it. If he wished to acquire Greek or Hebrew he must provide masters for himself. The bishop was to take care that the people should be instructed in the catechism; and no one was admitted to full membership with the church who did not know the Creed, the Lord's Prayer, and the Ten Commandments. The minister was allowed to take his sermon from the Book of Homilies. A singular regulation provided that a person who had been excluded from communion for notorious transgressions might remain in the church during the sermon, but must afterwards withdraw; if he resisted, and would not go out, divine service was to close. The old and the severest church penalty was retained, which compelled great offenders, and those especially who were guilty of fornication and adultery, to stand naked before the church door. The seven cathedrals of the kingdom were to be provided

with a modest staff of officials—the bishop, his com-
missary or chancellor, an assistant minister, the acting
rector of the church, a schoolmaster, a teacher of theology, a penitentiary, and a church warden. The
bishop was to be elected by the clergy, and a selected
number of the laity. The episcopal title was again
generally assumed under the reign of John, though not
enforced by canon.

We can see in these regulations the effort of the
bishop and the clergy to resist the innovations of the
king and to retain, and even to increase, the simplicity
in the performance of the services which prevailed
under Gustavus. But, as we shall see, these efforts
were of little avail. An opposite policy was adopted
by the successor of the archbishop. The venerable
friend of King Gustavus died two years after these regulations were made—regulations which seem not to
have been enforced, beyond the bounds of his own immediate jurisdiction.

Laurentius Petri Gothus made Abp. After the death of the archbishop, 1572, which
removed the greatest obstacle to his reaction-
ary policy, King John more openly proclaimed
and prosecuted his designs. He caused his own son-in-
law, Laurentius Petri Gothus, to be chosen archbishop.
The new primate was a man of compliant temper, and
by a devotion to the works of the Fathers, upon which
he held prelections in Upsala, had persuaded himself
that a system midway between Romanism and Protestantism was that which had prevailed in the primitive church, and should be adopted in Sweden. He
drew up and subscribed, and induced some of the clergy
to subscribe—for they were not enforced by synodical
action—seventeen articles in which the restoration of
convents, veneratien of the saints, prayers for the dead,

and most of the ceremonies of the old church, were approved. He was consecrated with full hierarchical pomp
in 1575. There was used on that occasion for the first
time the episcopal mantle, miter, and crosier, which the
Swedish bishops afterwards retained, although at that
time they were much opposed by the clergy. By the
king's express command the ceremony of anointing the
bishop was also performed. It was in the following year
that the Jesuits of whom I have spoken came to Stockholm. They were received without suspicion as good
Lutherans. As they were highly esteemed for their
learning, and the mass of the clergy were but little educated, the king required all of them that were in Stockholm to attend their lectures. The king caused them to
hold public disputations in which he himself took part,
and inveighed vehemently against the Pope, but allowed
himself to be easily confuted. Numerous secret con-
versions were effected. The scheme of the king seemed
about to succeed. But the Pope, Gregory XIII., began
to be impatient of these slow and secret proceedings,
and at the degree in which the king assumed to guide
and control the affairs of the church. When the king
proposed to the Pope that the priests should for the
present read inaudibly the invocations to saints, and
the prayers for the dead, the latter demanded that
such methods should be abandoned, and exhorted
the king, if he were earnest and conscientious in the
matter, to make a public profession of the Catholic
faith.

The Liturgy not univer- sally ac- cepted. The Liturgy which, as we have seen, was
constructed according to the views of the
king, under the direction of Peter Herbst,
his queen's chaplain, and the Jesuit Norvegus,
was published by the authority of the archbishop, who

.

assumed its authorship; and was also sanctioned by Erasmus, Bishop of Westeras. But it was not universally approved and adopted. The Duke Charles, when earnestly requested by the king to introduce it in the regions under his jurisdiction, peremptorily refused; and reminded him that according to their father's will they were bound not to make or allow any alteration in the established religion of the kingdom. The courtiers declared that the bishops and clergy were bound to obey the archbishop as their spiritual father, who, by the very nature of his office, was invested with patriarchal authority. The king issued a decree that henceforth the election of a bishop should not rest with the clergy of the diocese alone; but that the Archbishop and Archchapter of Upsala, should be co-electors. All ecclesiastical promotions were conditioned upon the acceptance of the Liturgy. The king required the ministers of Stockholm to send to him their opinion of it in writing. They replied, through Mr. Abraham, Rector of their High School, that it seemed to them that it must be the design, as it certainly was the tendency, of the introduction of the Liturgy, to restore Romanism. This stout answer brought down upon them the wrath of the king, and their dismissal from office, and the imprisonment of some of them. They replied that although they had subscribed the Liturgy in its first form, various additions had since been made to it, which they could not, with a good conscience, sanction. They expressed a willingness to appeal to and abide by the decisions of a free Synod called to consider the subject.

Accordingly a Synod was held at Stockholm in which all the clergy of Sweden, with the exception of those under the government of Duke Charles, were represented. The power of the king and the influence of the archbishop secured a majority in favor of the Liturgy. An article was adopted which prepared the way for the reception of the full Romish doctrine of a propitiatory sacrifice of Christ in the mass, by the assertion of an unbloody sacrifice. Mr. Abraham, and the clergy of Stockholm and the professors of Upsala, vigorously and boldly contested this position, and resisted the introduction of the Liturgy. They were immediately deposed and put in prison. The king found little difficulty in bringing the National Diet to sign the Liturgy and to pass a decree that whosoever should oppose the decisions of the Synod and refuse to accept it should be accounted enemies of the State. And with all this influence and these penalties in support of the action of the Synod and the Diet the king required three other eminent professors of Upsala, who were not present at the Synod, to give him their opinion concerning these measures in writing, and felt assured that they would be intimidated from giving an adverse answer. But they absolutely rejected the Liturgy, and the doctrinal decrees of the Synod; and argued at length against them on the authority of Luther and other eminent divines. They also appealed to the great Universities of Germany—Wittemberg, Leipsic, Helmstadt and Frankford—for their judgment in the matter. These all and earnestly condemned the Liturgy, and denounced it as a palpable device to reinstate the Church of Rome in its old supremacy in Sweden. These emphatic Protestant testimonies and demonstrations very considerably checked the progress of the Romeward movement.

The King's Embassy to the Pope. In the autumn preceding this Synod the king had sent Pontus de la Gardie and Peter Fechten on an embassy to the Pope. They were shipwrecked in the Baltic, and Fechten perished; but his colleague proceeded on his mission. John requested the Pope to enjoin the Catholic churches throughout the world to offer prayers for the restoration of the Catholic religion in the north of Europe, but not to specify Sweden by name. He begged that the cup should be given to the laity; that the bishops should be judged by the king in capital cases and accusations of treason; that no claims should be made on church estates that had been confiscated; that the college erected in Stockholm, where already secret instructions in Catholic doctrines were given, might receive the Papal confirmation, and the teachers be exempted for the present from wearing the monkish garb; that King Gustavus and King Eric and all the nobility who had died out of the communion of the church, should not be disturbed in their graves; that priests' marriages should be allowed, while celibacy should be encouraged and lauded as the better life; that the king might without sin join in the worship of the heretics, until the Catholic rites and services should be established. John assured the Pope that the way was prepared for the reinstatement of the Catholic worship by the restored dignity and splendor of the services, by the renewal of several abolished holy days, by the introduction of fast days and confession, by the restoration of convents, which had already begun, and by the education of several noble Swedish youths in Rome, Vienna, and other Catholic cities.

Mission of the Jesuit Cardinal, Anthony Possevin. The suggestions of King John were by no means satisfactory to the Pope. They allowed far too much power in ecclesiastical affairs to be exercised by the king, to be compatible with the Pope's claim to absolute, universal, unquestioned and unquestionable authority. Meanwhile, disguising his dissatisfaction, he dispatched Cardinal Possevin to Stockholm to work on the king's mind and bring him into full subjection to the Papal policy. In order to avoid a clamor among the people, the cardinal came not as a Nuncio—which he was in fact—from the Pope, but as the representative of the emperor. At Wadstena, in 1578, King John was secretly reconciled and brought into full communion with the Catholic Church, in the presence of the cardinal. From that period the proceedings of the king in favor of the Catholic Church, and against that which was established, become more open. No doubt could longer remain in the minds of the Protestants that the king was resolutely bent on the full restoration not only of the Catholic worship, but of the Papal power. The Bishop of Linkoping, Martin Olaveson, was stripped of his Episcopal robes publicly before the altar of his own cathedral, for having called the Pope Antichrist. His see was bestowed on the infamous Peter Carlson, Ordinary of Calmar, a parasite of Eric, who was popularly believed to have instigated the murder of the Sturés. All passages against the Pope were expelled from the Canticles. Luther's Catechism was banished from the schools. New silver shrines were provided for the relics of saints, which were brought out from the midst of the lumber to which they had been consigned for the last fifty years. An abridgement of Canon Law was drawn up for the guidance of the

Swedish Church. When the chair of the archbishop became vacant, in 1579, it was allowed to remain unoccupied for four years, in the hope that a Romanist might be appointed. Jesuits under manifold disguises entered the kingdom. John designed to employ them in the University, which he caused to be removed from Upsala to Stockholm, because of the stout resistance which its professors continued to offer to his designs. Many Swedish youths were sent out of the country to be educated in Jesuit schools.

Such was the rapid course of events and proceedings which seemed to make the restoration of Romanism probable, or a deadly struggle in the kingdom inevitable, when an event occurred which led to a reaction in the mind of the king, and to a pause in the aggressive measures which he had begun. The queen, Catherine Jagellonica, whose eminent virtues were admitted by all classes and parties in Sweden, died in 1583. From that time the advancing wave of Romish influence, which seemed about to overflow the whole land, had reached its highest point and began to recede. We should call it one of the insoluble mysteries of His government who is head over all things to His Church, that the orthodox faith of the Christian world under Constantine, and the Protestant faith of a kingdom under King John should be, or seem to be, dependent upon the fickle minds of two unworthy monarchs, did we not remember that neither does God govern the world, nor Christ the Church, by the annihilation of the freedom of the human will.

CHAPTER X.

Reaction in the Mind of the Abp. WHEN the archbishop was fully convinced that it was the design of the king to restore the Papal power in Sweden, he repented of his agency in sanctioning and assuming the authorship of the Liturgy. Nor did he fail to express to the king his regret at his reactionary measures, which had led to a system which was neither Protestantism nor Romanism, but which would inevitably end in the latter. Perceiving, however, that he exerted no influence with the king, and feeling that he had been used as a tool to further an object which he abhorred, and seeing that the cardinal, Possevin, had acquired absolute ascendency over the mind of the fickle king, he was brought, through jealousy of the cardinal and disapproval of the ends aimed at by the king, into a hostile attitude of mind, the blended result of mortification, indignation, and penitence. He now openly opposed the policy which he had been the chief agent to establish. He wrote, and published anonymously, a little book in which he unsparingly exposed the intrigues and denounced the errors of the Church of Rome. As he was a man of compliant, rather than an evil, nature, he bitterly bewailed his acquiescence in measures, whose real object he did not discern, which threatened to bring back the spiritual and temporal servitude from which Sweden had been emancipated by the heroic efforts of Gustavus. He died in the course of the following year under the frowns of the king, the hatred of the people, and the reproaches of his conscience.

Persecution of those who opposed the Liturgy. Notwithstanding the opposition of many of the most eminent men in the kingdom to the Liturgy and to measures which looked to the restoration of the Papacy, the king obstinately persisted in his policy. That opposition had appeared in an official form of so grave a character that it would seem calculated to make one even as conceited and obstinate as John to pause. When a diet was summoned to consider the question of a league between Poland and Sweden to resist the progress of the Russians in Livonia and Esthonia, that body devoted more attention to the religious condition of the country than to the object for which they were summoned. They represented to the king that as he had introduced many innovations in the religion of the country, it was commonly believed that he intended to restore Catholicism; and they therefore entreated him to declare in the presence of the States that the doctrine of the Church of Sweden was agreeable to that of the primitive Church; to take measures for banishing the Popish books that had been introduced into the kingdom; and to educate the prince Sigismund in the Protestant religion, in order that he might be more acceptable to the people, and that they might not fear that, on his accession, he would force them to become members of the Church of Rome. But King John had passed quite beyond any influence from remonstrances like these. It was at a period when he was most com-

pletely in subjection to Possevin, and most earnest in
his purpose to restore the Papacy. The opposition to
the Liturgy had found more or less emphatic expression from 1576 to the death of the queen, and everywhere it had been met with persecution, and in some
cases with the penalty of death. The king complains
in 1576 that in the diocese of Skara, Master Maurice
of Böne had endeavored to raise a great tumult against
it among councilors and nobles. The priest was examined by torture, and put to death with several of
his followers. In 1580 an order was given that the
revenues of those clergymen who did not observe the
Liturgy should be withheld; in 1582 it was enforced
under heavier penalties. Priests who refused obedience were deposed and imprisoned or driven into
exile. Nothing so irritated the king as the rejection of his Liturgy. He even inflicted personal violence on a clergyman of Stockholm, named Scheffer,
and so trampled upon him that the poor man's health
was broken for the remainder of his life.

Reaction in   After the death of the queen it was observed
the Mind of   that the zeal of the king for the restoration
the King.   of the Papacy began to cool. The with-
drawal of her influence on that behalf was not the
only, nor perhaps the most powerful, cause of this
change of feeling. Political resentments contributed
to the same result. He had solicited, and through the
mediation of the Pope he had hoped to obtain, the Neapolitan dukedoms of Bari and Rossini, on which his
wife had claims from her mother, *Bona Sforzia.* Neither had this expectation been fulfilled, nor had the
promise of the Pope to labor for the interests of Sweden
in the peace between Poland and Russia been kept.
On the contrary, the treaty negotiated under the me-

diation of Possevin confirmed the Polish claims to the Swedish possessions in Livonia. Not long after these events we find John so exasperated against the Pope that he actually began to persecute the Catholics. Laurence Forss, a minister of Stockholm who had become a Catholic, was deposed with the same degrading ceremonies which had been employed in the case of the Bishop of Linkoping for having called the Pope Antichrist. The Jesuits were banished from the realm, their new college in Stockholm abolished, and the instruction of its students assigned to Lutheran professors. By a proclamation all converts to the Catholic Church were threatened with exile, if they did not speedily recant. While the king was in this mood he turned his attention for a time to the Greek Church, and believed that by connecting himself with it he might still retain and enforce his beloved Liturgy. But when he found that the Greek Church was even less flexible in its forms than the Latin, and that no departures from her ritual would be allowed, he settled down on his original purpose of enforcing his own mongrel forms. His position was such as made it quite impossible for any large number of persons who had been either Protestants or Romanists to accept his system *ex animo*, although many would seemingly acquiesce in it, in order to escape punishment or acquire promotion.

Position and Character of Prince Sigismund. The young Prince Sigismund had been carefully trained by his mother in the Catholic faith. On her death bed she solemnly exhorted him to be faithful to his creed and to turn a deaf ear to all persuasions to apostatize. The prince, who had far more steadiness of character than his father, though with much less intellectual force, had accepted Catholicism with full conviction, and held it in the tight grasp with which narrow minds hold exclusive systems, and threw into it a fervor of zeal which became almost fanaticism. It was in vain that the senators and nobles of the kingdom endeavored to induce him to accept the Protestant faith. They made no impression upon him. The change in his father's policy after his mother's death seemed to render her principles and her character all the more sacred to him. When the nobles who attempted to influence him stated that by adhering to the Roman Church he would forfeit his right of succession to the crown, he answered that he preferred the kingdom of heaven to all the kingdoms of the earth. Dark indeed seemed the prospects of Protestantism in Sweden. A vascillating and arbitrary king, rooting out now the Romanism which he had fostered and repressing the Protestantism which was its only effective antagonist, in the vain attempt to establish a visionary *via media* of his own invention which was equally repugnant to both parties—such was the situation! Between two sharply defined systems, which differ from their foundation all the way up to their ultimate development, there can be no standing place, but only a gulf of separation. *Via media* in such a case is *via perditionis*. Add to this deplorable present, the prospect of a bigoted young Catholic king as the successor to the throne, and we may well believe that the hearts of all true Protestants must have had forebodings of new scenes of blood and sorrow. The only point of hope on which their eyes could rest was Duke Charles, whose decisive character and great abilities and determined resistance of the Papal propagandism in his provinces, seemed to furnish a pledge that when the inevitable battle between the two systems should commence, Protestantism would have in him a champion and leader not unworthy of his heroic parentage.

Hostile At- *In Reference to Temporal Interests.* We have *titude of* seen how treacherously King John violated *King John and Duke* the compact by which he and Duke Charles *Charles.* were to exercise an equal sovereignty. The anomalous relation of the two brothers, and the conflict of jurisdiction between the crown which claimed authority over all the kingdom, and the duke who asserted his independent sovereignty over the provinces assigned to him, led to many bitter conflicts and mutual recriminations. War would certainly have ensued between the brothers had not John been conscious that he would be supported by no partisans within the jurisdiction of Charles; and that Charles had some avowed and many more secret and earnest friends, who would rally at once around a banner on which the venerable name of Gustavus and the word Protestantism should be inscribed. That the claim of Charles was in conformity to the settlement made by Gustavus and sanctioned by the States, is clear. His independent jurisdiction was not to be interfered with, and when the emergencies of national politics called for the united action of all Sweden, this was to be obtained, not by the authority of the king over the domain of Charles, but by a general diet of the States gathered from every part of the kingdom. It was a system indeed which could not work without constant friction; but whether wise or unwise it was the supreme law of the land. The will of the king declared indeed on the one side that the princes should have no right to sever themselves or their fiefs from the crown of Sweden; that they were bound to be true to the king, and obliged to assist him in conflicts with foreign powers with the largest force which they could raise; but, on the other side, the king says that "the principalities are delivered up to them with all their appurtenances and advantages *as we have possessed the same on behalf of the crown without exception.*" He adds: "Our dear sons, as well he who comes into the throne and government, as the others with their heirs, shall in relation to those affairs on which the general welfare of the realm depends, undertake, transact, or conclude, nothing, be it peace or war or compacts or alliances, important to the State unless it be done with the counsel and assent of all the estates and divers of the chief men of the realm." It would be difficult to express a conjoint reign more distinctly, especially as each of the brothers is even allowed, in cases where manifest advantages can be gained for Sweden, and time does not allow a common deliberation, to follow his own resolution. In short, Charles was not the king's viceroy, but a sovereign prince with a more independent and looser relation to the sovereign power than that now held by the separate German kingdoms to the emperor of Germany.

In Reference to Religion. Even if differences between the brothers in reference to secular interests could have been adjusted, it was impossible that Charles could be at cordial peace with John, so long as the latter persisted in demanding that he should accept and enforce his Liturgy. Charles constantly replied that he would not depart by a hair's breadth from the doctrine and polity and ritual which had been laid down, after God's Word, by his father, and which he had solemnly enjoined his sons to observe and defend. All negotiations on this subject were entirely fruitless. When the king ordered the use of his Liturgy throughout the kingdom,

Charles forbade it within his principality, and adhered to the Kirk's Ordinances of 1571. He was sustained in this position by his clergy and people; and he protected and favored those who were persecuted by the king, and fled to him; "because," he writes to the king, "we profess ourselves of the religion by which they hold." The Bishop of Linkoping, whom John had deprived, was nominated by Charles pastor of Nykoping. The theological professors of Upsala, five of whom at different times had been deprived and imprisoned on account of the Liturgy, enjoyed his protection; and one of them, Peter Jonson, was raised to the Bishopric of Strengness. The preachers of Stockholm who rejected the Liturgy also fled to him and were favorably received. Many retracted the assent to the new service which they had given under pressure and threats, after they had become convinced that John intended, or that his measures would lead to, the restoration of Romanism. Reports were circulated through all the kingdom that the late archbishop had died in agonies of conscience. In the year 1587 so numerous had the refugees into Charles' principality become that the king threatened war, unless his Liturgy were adopted, and these fugitives sent back. Charles calmly replied that he would leave the question of the acceptance of the Liturgy to the clergy; and he made no promise of the restoration of the refugees. The Liturgy was condemned, as Charles was sure it would be, at a synod held at Strengness. The king vented his wrath upon them in a violent letter, in which he called the clergy unlearned smatterers, ass-heads, Satanists, and declared that they should be treated as outlaws throughout his dominions.

The *Red Book* of John, as his Liturgy was called, was thus the cause of the most perilous misunderstanding between the brothers; and so violent was the strain, that war ever seemed upon the point of breaking out. Men saw in Charles the faithful son and representative of Gustavus, whose name was more and more venerated as time, and the contrast with his successors, manifested his greatness. They accepted him also as a champion of the reformation, not only from political and patriotic motives, but also from profound religious convictions. It was in fact the same struggle of principles, though under somewhat different forms and watchwords, which was convulsing Bohemia and Austria; and seemed about to culminate in the restoration of the Papacy over all the countries of Europe, except England and Scotland. When we look forward a few years and see how on the labors of that great hero, Gustavus Adolphus,—the noble knight, the consummate general, the pure and earnest Christian,—the salvation of periled Protestantism in Europe depended, and how by his victories the thirty years' war resulted in securing the rights of Protestant States, and remember that it was the fidelity of Charles which made it possible for Adolphus to succeed to a Protestant throne and kingdom, we perceive that we are not dealing with an insignificant struggle in a small and distant kingdom, whose issue would not affect the great interests of Europe and the world; but we recognize that we are spectators of an arena where champions for the truth are in the process of training for a victorious struggle which will entitle them to the gratitude and admiration of all succeeding time.

John's second Marriage, and its Consequences. In less than a year after the death of the queen, King John married Gunilla Bielke, a maiden of but sixteen years of age, daughter of a counselor of state, John Bielke. The marriage was celebrated with great pomp, in Feb-

ruary, 1585, at the castle of Westeras.   The young wife
favored, as far as she could without incurring the wrath
of the king, the opponents of the Liturgy.   But not
even her great influence could deter the king from per-
sisting in pressing it upon the kingdom.   It had become a question in which he felt that his royal prerogative and kingly dignity were involved.   But inasmuch
as their marriage had offended all his kindred, and increased the alienation of Charles, the king became
seriously alarmed lest his enemies might by the aid
of his brother overthrow him; and was thus led to
court and to bestow new favors upon the nobility in
order that he might rely upon their support.   The
policy was, in good measure, successful; for the courtiers and nobility were well aware that they could hope
for no favoritism, or increase of their privileges, from
the stern and austere Charles, if he should ascend the
throne.   And yet, notwithstanding this new rally of
the favored nobility to his support, the apprehensions
of John, in consequence of the vehement disapproval
of his marriage by all his kindred, were rather increased than diminished.   His children by his former
marriage, Sigismund and Ann, saw with no pleasant
feeling one of the waiting maids of their mother advanced to the position of their queen and step-mother.
The sisters of John wrote bitter letters to him on the
subject; and received from him and the spirited young
queen defiant and bitter letters in reply.   Charles had
endeavored to dissuade the king from this marriage,
and refused to be present at its celebration.   And so
the alienation of the brothers was constantly on the
increase.   John was so nervously anxious about the
designs of his brother that when, in 1585, he passed
through a portion of his principality, he hastened

through it under the apprehension that he might be
captured; and refused to allow Sigismund to engage
in hunting lest Charles might lay an ambush for him.
Charles showed the same distrust of his brother by refusing to attend the Diet of Wadstena without a safe-
conduct. It was given, and Charles attended the Diet;
but the new influence of the king with the nobility enabled him to impose some restrictions upon the authority of Charles, to which he was either obliged or
felt it policy to succumb. But upon the subject of the
Liturgy he refused to yield, according to the language
which he had formerly used to his brother, by a single
hair's breadth.

*Election of
Sigismund
to the Throne
of Poland.*   *Election at first declined.* On the death of
Stephen, King of Poland, his widow Anne,
the aunt of Sigismund, at once labored for
his election. She was aided in this effort
by delegates sent by King John to second the scheme
—Eric Sparré and Eric Brahe. The Estates of Sweden
were not consulted in the matter. While the negotiation was in progress Duke Charles gave, as he was
asked to do, renewed pledges that he would remain
true to Sigismund as heir to the Swedish throne; and
only made the reservation that Esthonia should not
be ceded to Poland, but should be reserved for himself.
There was no difficulty in the matter of religion; for
Poland required that their king should be a Catholic,
and Sigismund would be nothing else. But other conditions to the acceptance of the throne were displeasing
to John and to his son. These were—that Esthonia
should revert to Poland; that Sigismund, after his
father's death, should be king of Sweden, and trans-
mit it to his male heir; that in cases of alleged necessity he might go to Sweden, if Poland gave her consent;

that he should keep a fleet, at his own charge, in
Sweden (when he became king) which he should lend
to the Poles when they were at war with Russia—that
he might bring foreign troops to his aid in war only
on condition that he should himself pay them. He
should not make use of Swedish counselors in Poland
and should have only Poles and Lithuanians for his
guards, and give fiefs and offices in the kingdom to
them alone. These high demands, coupled with the
fact that, while they were yet under consideration, the
Archduke Maxmilian of Austria was elected by a mi-
nority party of Poles which it became necessary to re-
press by force of arms, and the fear of committing his
only son and heir to so turbulent a kingdom, induced
King John, with the glad assent of Sigismund, to reject the proffered crown. But his unscrupulous agent,
Sparré, secured his consent by disguising from him,
and even denying, that the surrender of Esthonia was
one of the conditions of the election.

The Statutes of Calmar. The evils of the subservi-
ency of John to the nobles, which he had shown in
order to fortify himself against Charles, and of the renewal of their privileges, which had so often nullified
the power of the throne, and which it was the life-work
of Gustavus to destroy, now became apparent. A new
code of statutes, drawn up by the accomplished and
subtle Sparré, is introduced by exaggerated exaltation
of the position and privileges of the nobility. It is
declared that to the nobility of Sweden belong high
reverence and honor, since they have ever held the
chief rank after kings, from whom many of them are
descended and some of whom have been elected to
the throne. It is therefore to be understood that
hereafter there are certain kinds of court service which

they shall not be called upon or expected to render, and not allowed to render even if they profess a willingness or a desire to do so. They are not to be employed as guards and lackeys and servitors in the royal palace. Thus it is seen that, in order to secure a defense against Charles, King John had come into bondage to a proud and overbearing nobility.

Purport of the Calmar Statutes. After this ominous introduction the statutes proceed to declare the objects to be accomplished through their enactment. The number and minuteness of the conditions and regulations on the part of both kingdoms, with a view to the maintenance respectively of their rights and privileges, show distinctly the consciousness of both parties of the extreme difficulty on the part of a conscientious or bigoted Catholic king of one country to govern satisfactorily another kingdom which was decidedly and resolutely Protestant. Their arrangements and conditions proved that it was regarded as extremely difficult; and the event showed, as it has often elsewhere been shown, that it was impossible.

The council of Sweden prevailed upon John to insist upon certain conditions to be observed by Sigismund, when he should become king, which it is evident that the latter, as a faithful Catholic, could not intend to perform. When Sigismund, as king, should come into Sweden he should not bring with him any Romish priests; and he should grant the Romish priesthood in the kingdom no greater privileges than they already enjoyed. In Poland he should not oppress any Protestant officers in his service on account of their religion; in Sweden he should not advance any of the Poles to offices and dignities. He should not allow any innovations to be made in the doctrines and ceremonies

of the Church of Sweden. The hospitals established
by his father on Protestant foundations should not be
changed. The extreme condition was exacted, that no
worship, public or private, but the established Protestant worship, should be allowed. On his return to Poland he should take with him the priests that were in
his train; and while they were in Sweden they should
not be allowed to engage in any instruction or service
or affairs, outside the palace. The Pope should not be
permitted to install any bishops or establish any bishoprics in Sweden; and that his coronation should take
place at Upsala and be performed by the archbishop.
These ecclesiastical conditions were followed by those
that were political and secular.. They were drawn up
with equal care and minuteness, with a view to maintain the independence and the liberties of Sweden.

*The Commencement of the Reign of Sigismund in
Poland.* The collisions and misunderstandings which
were inevitable, in a settlement which contained so
many expedients to reconcile opposing interests, immediately occurred. The Poles insisted upon the surrender of Esthonia and a part of Livonia, which had
been assigned to them by the commissioners Sparré
and Brahe, and the knowledge of which had been kept
from King John and Sigismund. The new king, after
most unpromising dissensions with his subjects, at
length yielded the point only under a protest, which
contemplated a future revision of the treaty. The
commissioners feared to return to Sweden and in-
cur the loudly-vented wrath of John at the deception which had been passed upon him. King Sigismund made a humble excuse to his father for having
consented to this article; but assured him that it was
only a temporary concession which he would soon find

means to revoke. The poor young king was so disgusted with the turbulent character of his subjects, and
of what he called their insupportable pride, that he
conveyed to his father, through the messenger that carried his letter, his resolution to give his sister Anne in
marriage to the Archduke Ernest of Austria, and to
yield to him the kingdom, and return to Sweden.

The Liturgy enforced anew. King John persisted in pressing his Liturgy
upon the kingdom, with a violence in which
there was blended the wounded pride of an
author, with the arrogance of a despot. When the
clergy in the principality of Charles formally and
unanimously condemned it, he prepared a proclamation, which he ordered to be posted conspicuously
throughout the kingdom, in which he accused these
ecclesiastics of rebellion, heresy, and treason. His
temper had become ungovernable, and he laid upon it
no restraint in his private or public proceedings. He
called the clergy who had condemned his Liturgy, dis-
ciples of the devil, and burned all the books which Mr.
Abraham had published against the Liturgy. The
clergy appealed to Duke Charles, and he assured them
of his approbation and of his purpose to support them
to the full extent of his power. The clergy replied
with spirit to these denunciations of the king; and referred to the Scriptures, the Augsburg Confession, and
Luther's Catechism, in proof of their orthodoxy. They
also wrote a dignified exposition of their views, and an
appeal to all the clergy and nobility to aid them in
sustaining the faith and order of the Church, as they
were settled by the great Gustavus. This proceeding
so alarmed and exasperated the king that he determined to bring back Sigismund from Poland to assist him in resisting the rising spirit of dissatisfaction

throughout the kingdom. But if that purpose had been accomplished, it would have served rather to increase than to quell the opposition which his arbitrary measures now encountered. In his anger and alarm he required all the clergy of Sweden—and he was generally obeyed, except in the domains of Charles—to bind themselves to him by an oath that they would be faithful to him and not in any way assist Charles, if he should revolt. This writing was signed by all the clergy of Stockholm except one, and he was deprived, and treated with great indignity and violence.

Conference between Kings John and Sigismund. The disposition of the king to rule alone, uncontrolled and even uninfluenced by his counselors and estates, constantly increased. When his council remonstrated with him on the extravagance and disorder of his household, at a time when the resources of the kingdom were strained to the utmost by the war with Russia, which had continued during all his reign, the king was much offended, and would take no steps at reformation which should seem to be in obedience to their suggestions. Disgusted with his position, and alarmed at the attitude of the subjects of Charles, and longing for a sight of his son Sigismund, the king determined to meet and confer with him at Reval. The impatience of John was such that he would not wait for his military escort, and against the remonstrances of his counselors, who earnestly endeavored to dissuade him from the journey, he embarked early in July with his queen and a newborn son, and reached Reval two weeks before Sigismund arrived. It was rumored and believed by the council that John intended to bring back Sigismund to Sweden, and not allow him again to return to Poland. The kings spent a month together

at Reval. There bitter dissensions and frequent bloody
conflicts broke out between the Swedes and Poles who
were in the trains of the two kings. An irruption of
Tartars into Poland furnished occasion to the counselors of Sigismund for an imperative demand that he
should immediately return to his kingdom and his
duties. On the other hand the Swedish council sought
to lay before John the remonstrances determined upon.
at Upsala against bringing Sigismund into Sweden.
John refused to see the lords who came to lay this
protest before him. Their remonstrance painted in
vivid colors the dreadful condition of the country,
the result of an almost continuous war of twenty-
eight years with Russia, and of the reckless extravagance of the king and court. Famine prevailed in
various sections of the country. Peace was the first
necessity of the kingdom; and Russia was now disposed to enter into negotiations. If Sigismund should
abandon Poland and return to Sweden, as did Henry of
Valois to France, then would irritated Poland unite with
Russia against Sweden, and she would be ruined and
conquered and divided. This paper was signed by
sixty-one names of the most eminent men in the
kingdom. When the soldiers who were at Stockholm
heard how John had refused to listen to the remonstrances of the council, they assembled in high excitement before the royal palace, and threw down their
colors, and declared with loud oaths that they would
no longer serve his majesty, if he should bring back
King Sigismund into Sweden. The crisis was too
alarming to allow the king to carry out his design.
But it was a bitter disappointment, which left rankling
hatred in his heart against the principal counselors
who had signed the memorial, and especially against

those lords who had attempted to present it to him
at Reval. The two kings reluctantly parted and never
saw each other again. John now began to find that
the power which he had given to the nobles to be
used for his defense against Charles, could as readily
be directed against himself.

King John's Reconciliation with Charles. The now critical relation of John with his
counselors and the nobility made it neces-
sary for him to be reconciled to Charles. It
became all the more imperative from the fact
that the nobles and all Sweden observed that while all
was confusion and waste in the court and administration of the king, the principality of Charles was comparatively prosperous, and all its affairs conducted
with system and economy. Hence Charles was rein-
stated in all the privileges and rights connected with
his principality, which at the suggestion of the king
had been curtailed by the nobility at the Diet of
Wadstena. He resided for the most at Stockholm;
and in fact became the real administrator of the
kingdom. John acknowledged that more was now
accomplished in three days than formerly in as many
months. Chafing under a sense of his comparative insignificance, and baffled in his attempts at an un-
checked arbitrary rule, and exasperated with the lords
who had so peremptorily and effectively protested
against the return of Sigismund to Sweden, King
John did little else than study how he might have
his revenge on those lords and counselors who had
defeated his cherished plan, and had treated him with
scant respect. Selecting the names of six of the most
obnoxious of the lords, for what he termed "the revolt in Reval," he issued his commands that their fiefs
should be sequestered, that none of them should be

admitted to any of the royal castles, and that they should repair to Stockholm to answer for their treason. The Estates were convoked, and the six lords arraigned. On making certain acknowledgments they were permitted to retain their estates; but they signed a secret document in which they protested that they had committed no crime, but had only exercised the privileges and the duties of faithful counselors of the king and kingdom. But the vindictive king still continued to urge against them his charge of disloyalty and treason. They were imprisoned for two years; and during all that period were subjected to repeated examinations. In urging on this charge, to which he had added still another, to the effect that they were engaged in a conspiracy with many others to exclude Sigismund from the throne of Sweden, King John made the most exorbitant claims to absolute authority. It was in vain that the wives of these accused lords, and Sigismund himself, pleaded for them with the king. The appeal of Sigismund was both politic and just. "Even if they were not altogether guiltless," he wrote, "yet should his majesty let grace stand for law, and ponder how grievously it would fall out for his son to come into a government where widows and orphans, in part not distantly related to the royal house, would cry vengeance upon him as the author of their woes." All appeals were in vain. The implacable king would have his revenge. The lords, and many of their alleged accomplices, were imprisoned and subjected to heavy penalties.

Death of King John. The king died in the castle of Stockholm on the 17th of November, 1592, in the fifty-fifth year of his age. During the last year of his life he suffered the penalty that falls on tyrants, of a dread and suspicion of all around him. There is nothing in his character to admire. He was learned, indeed, and possessed of more talent than ordinarily belongs to kings; but he was mean, suspicious, jealous, cruel, negligent, indolent, and profuse. Honest History must write over his grave the simple epitaph: "*A mean man and a bad king.*"

CHAPTER XI.

WE no sooner enter upon the story of what is called the reign of King Sigismund in Sweden, than we are at once ushered into a scene of conflict which arose from the struggle of the two systems of Romanism and Protestantism for supremacy. As mutual toleration was at that time impossible, perpetual collision was inevitable between a king whose conscience constrained him to force Romanism upon his subjects, and a Protestant people equally resolute and conscientious in their resistance to such an attempt. If John was able to weaken the foundation of the institutions of Sweden based on the Reformation, much more aggressive and destructive measures might be anticipated from a king so devoted to the Papacy and the Jesuits, that even John, in his own temporary surrender to Rome, felt that his son went too far, and advised him to be aware of those Fathers who were accustomed to keep one foot in the pulpit and the other in the council room.

Position of Charles in Sweden. Charles had in fact conducted the government of Sweden for the last two years of King John's reign. As the king had made no definite arrangements for the administration of the kingdom after his death, it was natural that it should remain with Charles. The duke advised King Sigismund of his father's death, and consulted him upon the measures to be taken for carrying on the war with Russia. The six counselors deprived and imprisoned by John, were pardoned and recalled—a measure that was agreeable to the king. He also set at liberty all persons who were confined on account of the Liturgy, or for political causes. A letter soon came from the king confirming Charles in the government, until he should be able to visit Sweden.

So far, on the surface, all was well. But the politic and able duke was aware that already intrigues were going on in Finland and elsewhere in behalf of the Papacy. He therefore entered into a compact with the council that they should obey him in everything which the interests of religion and the independence of the kingdom demanded—but without prejudice to their fealty to the king. Both Charles and his council could consistently make this reservation of fealty to the king because they did not hold that this fealty required them to acquiesce in the overthrow of the legally established Protestantism and independence of the country. King Sigismund of course saw what was the animus and meaning of this language, and was accustomed to call it Charles's bird-net. The duke assured the council that he would engage in no important affairs without their advice and consent. That this pledge of obedience, saving the prerogatives of the king, might sometimes carry the council further than they desired to go, soon appeared. The clergy of Stockholm pressed for the calling of a synod, promised by King John in 1590, for the adjustment of religious disputes. The council thought that the mat-

ter should be adjusted by a joint commission of their
own body and of the clergy. But Charles well knew
that in so small a body reactionary influences would
be more likely to prevail than in a large assembly.
He therefore demanded that there should be a general
Diet of the kingdom; and he carried his point. King
Gustavus had secured Protestantism and freedom for
Sweden, and these must at all hazards and sacrifices
be preserved. He declared—and the statement must
have been most offensive to Sigismund—that he only
could be regarded as the true hereditary king of
Sweden who preserved them unimpaired. They had
now a king whose conscience was directed by the
Pope; they should therefore renew their loyalty to
and declare in unmistakable words and acts their purpose to defend and secure, the hard-won, but inestim-
able blessings, obtained and transmitted to them by
the great Gustavus. It was under the influence of
this bold and animating manifesto that the Diet met
in Upsala, on the 25th of February, 1593.

The Diet of Upsala. Deputies from every part of Sweden except
Finland come to the Diet. Finland was
under the government of a partisan of Sigismund. It was
for Sweden an unusually large assembly. There were
present the duke with his council, four bishops, above
three hundred clergy, many of the nobles and representatives of the burgesses and peasants. A very
enthusiastic and resolute spirit prevailed. Nicholaus
Bothniensis, Professor of Theology at Upsala, although
a young man, was elected speaker. This was a manifestation of homage to the steadfastness with which
the Upsala professors had resisted the Liturgy; and it
was a plain sign of the spirit that animated the Diet.
They decreed that the Scriptures were the sole rule of

faith; and they considered and sanctioned all the articles of the unmutilated Augsburg Confession.   Thereupon Peter Jonson, recently consecrated Bishop of
Strengness, rose and inquired whether all present
assented to and would defend these articles of faith,
and abide by them even if called upon to suffer for it.
All replied that they pledged all they had in this
world, goods and life, in their defense.   Then the
speaker exclaimed, " Then is Sweden become one man,
and all of us have one God."   In view of the persecu-
tions which they had suffered under John, and those
much more severe which Sigismund, if he should obtain
ascendency, would inflict, the spectacle of this representation of a *nation*, and not of an ecclesiastical synod
alone, entering into such a religious compact, is a truly
noble one.   The event proved that, on the part of the
great majority of its members, it was a compact sincerely entered into, and faithfully maintained.

The changes in church ceremonies and doctrines
which had been introduced under the former reign
were abolished.   Luther's Catechism was adopted as
the groundwork of religious instruction and Laurence
Peterson's manual the formulary of divine service.
The bishops who had supported the Liturgy were
now the first and most earnest to renounce it.   They
requested of the Council of State the return of their
written engagements to support the Liturgy.   Some of
the council promised it; but Charles, well knowing
Episcopal pliancy, took care that they should be preserved in the archives of the Chancery.   Several of the
lords addressed earnest exhortations to the clergy to
stand firm hereafter on their privileges, and to be faithful to their pledges.   They complained that John had
forced into the ministry as his pliant agents in support

of his Liturgy, not only unlearned men, but often marriage breakers, thieves, perjurers, homicides, tipplers,
and leaders of vicious lives; and that only those who
supported the Liturgy were advanced to high benefices
in the Church, and that such men had been thrust into
the Episcopate by the arbitrary will of the king, without a canonical election by the clergy. They declared
therefore that if the Liturgy were not abolished before
the arrival of King Sigismund, the kingdom would be
in the condition of one who should attempt to carry a
light in a violent storm. All these proceedings leave
an impression that the nobility and commons had been
more faithful, and were now more in earnest in maintaining the Protestant faith than the clergy.

Position of Charles in the Diet. Charles took no part in the deliberations of
the diet. But, of course, his influence in it
must have been great. There seems to have
been no less moderation than firmness in their proceedings. No one was proscribed for having acquiesced
in the Liturgy. Only one minister, John Paulson of
Stockholm, was deprived. He had been so factious
and violent that King John himself had suspended
him. Charles subscribed the decrees of the Diet, and
did not disguise his disgust at the council for not
having declared themselves long before. He was indeed inclined to, although there is no proof that he
had as yet adopted, the tenets of the Reformed Church.
His first wife was a sister of the Elector Palatine; and
Charles was devoted to her and very friendly with all
her family. And now the bishops who had subscribed
to and enforced the Liturgy, in their new-born zeal
for pure Lutheranism, and probably with a view to rebuke the rumored sacramentarian views of Charles, were
very earnest to secure decrees against Zwinglians and

Calvinists as heretics.   The speaker, no doubt discerning the object of the bishops, refused to put the motion.   But they persisted and carried it, and secured the assent of Charles which was given in phrases more energetic than choice.   Charles was very angry at what he regarded as a personal rebuke.   In a confidential letter to the archbishop and professors of Upsala, he afterwards declared: "We are now defamed by the clergy as if we countenanced the doctrine of Calvin and Zwingle. But we will profess ourselves bound to no man's person, Christ excepted, neither Luther, Calvin, or Zwingle, but to God's Word alone."   His fault, so it would be regarded by the more intolerant clergy, was, not that he manifested any opposition to, or any want of reverence for, Luther, but that he did not sufficiently hate Calvin and Zwingle.

Importance of the Diet of Upsala.   The proceedings of the Diet of Upsala were not only most memorable in the history of Sweden, but of immense moment to the cause of Protestantism in Europe.   The Church of Sweden celebrates the anniversary of this diet every century with the same enthusiasm with which Germany celebrates the birthday of Luther.   It secured, after further struggles, the Reformation in Sweden, and, through Gustavus Adolphus, rescued it from extinction in Germany and other countries.   For many years a sermon was preached in all the churches in commemoration of the Sunday after the 19th of February, 1592, on which day Sigismund was compelled to acknowledge the Acts of the Diet of Upsala.   All the sermons were preached from the same text—a text which reminded the people of the fact that they had been, and could continue to be, prosperous and blessed only as they were faithful to God and to his truth.   The text of these sermons was the Second of Chronicles xv. 1, 2: "And the Spirit of God came upon Azariah the son of Oded: And he went out to meet Asa, and said unto him, Hear ye me, Asa, and all Judah and Benjamin; The Lord is with you, while ye be with him; and if ye seek him, he will be found of you; but if ye forsake him, he will forsake you."

Proceedings in Poland. The proceedings of the Polish Diet on the question of King Sigismund's visit and relation to Sweden, was marked by even more than the usual violence of Polish assemblies. At length it was agreed that Sigismund should be provided with means to visit his kingdom of Sweden, on the condition that he should make a satisfactory arrangement of the dispute between the two kingdoms in reference to Esthonia. Olaf Swerkerson, an intermediary between Charles and Sigismund, assured the former that the king would uphold the laws, liberties, and rights of his native land; and that he would show neither affection nor hatred to any man on account of his religion; but that he could not and would not sanction the decrees of Upsala passed during his absence.

But these general assurances were not satisfactory to the Swedes. They desired from Sigismund before he should leave Poland more explicit and favorable declarations, confirmed by guarantee, upon which they could rely. Accordingly, Thure Bielke, a man personally agreeable to Sigismund, was sent to Poland with a warrant in which the demands and expectations of Sweden were detailed, together with a copy of the Acts of the Diet of Upsala. These documents were ordered to be read in all the churches of the kingdom, in order to keep the heart of the people up to their duty in the crisis that was impending. Two eminent

nobles, Nicholas Bielke and Eric Sparre, were sent with
a fleet to Dantzic to meet the king and escort him into
Sweden.

But sinister rumors reached Sweden before the arrival of the king. It was reported that a Papal Legate
had arrived at Warsaw, with a command from the Pope
that he should restore the Church in his hereditary dominions, and that he had brought a subsidy in money
for the undertaking; that the imperial envoy used the
same language; and that the Legate was to follow Sigismund to Sweden and crown him there, in violation
of the compact between the two kingdoms; that Sigismund, in the course of his journey, had laid an interdict on the Evangelical Churches of Thorn and Elbing;
and that a fear of a similar proceeding at Dantzic had
led to popular tumults in that city. These rumors created much apprehension in the kingdom. Added to
these causes of disquiet was the attitude of the resolute
and turbulent governor of the important province of
Finland, Clas Fleming. The duke wrote to him that
he should admit no man into the castle of Abo without
an order from him and the Council of State. Fleming
replied that he had but one master in his government,
and that was King Sigismund. In a letter to Poland
he subscribed his name with additions, in which he
boldly announced his defiance of Charles and his determined loyalty to the king: "Clas Fleming, free
baron of Wilk, Marshal, High Admiral, and General,
who has now too many rulers, though he guides himself by only one, who is called King Sigismund. Come,
my mates, to command me too, and see if I do not
knock them on the head."

Arrival of Sigismund in Sweden. Notwithstanding the unsatisfactory nature of the preliminary proceedings between Charles and the king, the latter embarked on the fleet sent from Finland to Dantzic and landed in Stockholm on the 30th of September, 1593. Charles took his stand on the castle bridge to receive the king. The newly-elected archbishop, Abraham Angerman, who had been persecuted by John because of his determined opposition to the Liturgy, was appointed to welcome the king. This arrangement, significant of Charles's resolute purpose to keep Protestantism in the foreground, was very offensive to Sigismund and to the Legate, Malaspina. The king wrote complaining of it to Charles: "It is singular that Master Abraham, who had fallen into disgrace with our late father, should now be the person to receive us in the name of all the clergy." After an outburst of indignation against Clas Fleming, addressed to the king, and with a stern and independent bearing towards him, which clearly intimated his distrust, and gave warning that he was not to be intimidated or won, Charles retired to his principality and committed to the council the business of negotiation with the king.

Immediately collisions and disagreements occurred. Sigismund would not confirm the Acts of the Synod of Upsala, nor would he accept the new archbishop. The Jesuits and the clergy of Stockholm began to preach against each other. The king demanded the transfer of a church in a former monastery of Franciscans to the Catholics, and enforced a burial there with the Catholic ritual. This occasioned a conflict, and the shedding of blood in the church itself. The king sullenly kept aloof from the Swedish counselors, and surrounded himself with Roman partisans, and refused to receive

a deputation of the Protestant clergy. In reply to the
council, who pressed upon him certain pledges previous
to his coronation, he haughtily expressed his surprise
at their presumption, and reminded them of the differ-
ence between an hereditary and an elective monarchy.
As he succeeded to a kingdom the prevailing religion
of which was different from his own, he would leave
those who professed it unmolested; but he would insist
that those subjects which were of his faith should have
equal privileges with the majority.

Second Diet It was in this spirit of mutual exasperation
of Upsala. that both parties repaired to Upsala, where
the States were assembled to celebrate at once the en-
tombment of John and the coronation of Sigismund.
The obsequies of John were celebrated with great pomp;
but the Papal Legate was turned out of the procession,
and the Jesuits forbidden to enter the church on the
penalty of death. Charles took no part in the solem-
nity; but he was there with three thousand men, foot
and horse, whom he quartered on his hereditary possessions in the neighborhood. He said to the Estates
—" I part not from you; if Sigismund will be your king
he must fulfill your requests." He told the king that
no coronation should be permitted until the demands
and pledges required were given. When he proceeded
to the castle to make this announcement in person to
the king; he was accompanied by the council and nobility, and vast crowds of the applauding people. The
order of the peasants in the diet offered Charles the
crown; but he sternly commanded them to be silent.
It was a great crisis, and it was evident that the resolute and subtle Charles was equal to it.

Affairs seemed to be in what, in modern phrase,
would be called a dead-lock. The court labored to

bribe and disunite the Estates. Rumors were current,
and were afterwards confirmed, that an attempt was to
be made upon the life of Charles; but no charge was
made then or since that Sigismund was privy to the
design. Charles redoubled his vigilance and increased
his military force. In this period of painful suspense a
most impressive scene took place in the diet. The
whole assembly fell upon their knees and united in
prayer; and in that attitude vowed and pledged themselves to each other, at every hazard and every cost, to
uphold the decrees of the former Diet of Upsala. Under the impulse of that enthusiastic proceeding they
were ready to enact, as they did, very decided measures. They decreed that no Catholic should henceforth
be permitted to hold a civil office in Sweden. Whoever should embrace the Catholic faith, or permit his
children to be educated therein, should forfeit the right
of citizenship; Catholics might reside in the kingdom
if they conducted themselves peaceably; but no Catholic service should be performed except in the king
chapel. This was all that the king could obtain. An
when the duke, wearied with the delays and irritate
at the intrigues of the king, peremptorily announce
to him that unless he should give a decisive answer in
twenty-four hours, he would dissolve the diet and sen
its members home, he was obliged to yield. We may
be sure that it was a bitter necessity; and that there
could have been no sincerity in his extorted assent.
The *Te Deum* was sung by the States as upon occasions
of great military victories. The new archbishop wa
confirmed by the king. But to another bishop—the
bishop of Westeras—was assigned the service of coronation. The Jesuits were not permitted to be present.
When the king took the oath he allowed his hand to

drop; but Charles reminded him that he must hold
it upright until the conclusion of the pledge; and the
king obeyed. One would have supposed that these
events—this demonstration of the substantial unity of
the people in the Protestant faith, and of their firm
purpose to maintain it, and this taste of the quality of
his uncle Charles—would have sufficed to convince the
young king that his attempt to reintroduce Romanism
into Sweden could not possibly succeed.

The King faithless to his Pledges. The story of the king's evasion and viola-
lation of the solemn pledges which he made
at his coronation is found in manuscript,
among the papers of Adolphus Gustavus. No one
could be better informed on the subject than he; and
he has told the story, considering the temptations to
violent and indignant denunciations which he must
have experienced, with commendable moderation.

"Sigismund was slow in confirming all lay and
clerical privileges; and as he promised with hesitancy,
so he kept to it no longer than between Upsala and
Stockholm. He was hardly arrived at the capital,
when he made the Count Eric Brahe (a Catholic) to
be governor there, which was one of the highest offices
in the kingdom. Malaspina, the evil thorn that stuck
in the king's foot, made him halt sorely in his promises. Popish schools and Popish churches were erected;
around Stockholm divine service was interrupted by
disturbances; men were obliged to go armed to the
church, complaint thereof was made to the king, but
little good was thereby effected. Moreover the king's
counselors found it good to fish in troubled waters.
Sweden must be stirred up to civil discords that one
heretic might be extirpated by another. The king
hastened to Poland. Here all was to remain in dis-

order and confusion, no one bound to obey another, that the more speedily among so many magnates (for every province had its lieutenants), mischiefs might spring up. But as the majesty of the realm of Sweden was by God's blessing succored and defended to this day, so that it was never transferred to another monarchy, but by Swedish valor was preserved to this country and nation, so too were now found men who would not allow this design of the king to be effected. The council which was in Stockholm protested against him, that it was not competent for him to remove the kingly government out of the land; he should appoint a government within the realm who should manage its affairs. They also gave Charles, who lay sick at Nycoping, to understand this. The king indeed made out, though without good will, a warrant wherein with few words my father was empowered to manage the administration, with the council of state; but the lieutenants of the provinces were enjoined to pay this government no regard. Thus they did whatever they wished. To the people, who (in Sweden especially) were accustomed to law and justice, it appeared strange that they were treated so ill by the lieutenants; and as the people are beside prone to complain, so when they found themselves oppressed they ran in crowds to Stockholm where they were wont to find redress. The government would gladly have had from Sigismund a better warrant and fuller instructions, after which they might have ruled the people and realm for the king's behoof, which also while the king was in Stockholm was sufficiently promised; yet it was deferred from day to day, until the king was ready to sail, and no other could be obtained, whence all the disorder afterwards flowed."

The King-dom after Sigismund's Departure. It was the policy of Sigismund to leave Sweden in such an unsettled state that his intervention might become necessary to restore order; and that he might thus govern it according to his will, and reintroduce Romanism. When he found however that the nobility could not be won to sanction such a policy, in order to diminish the power of Charles he adopted the system that had prevailed under the settlement of Calmar, when Sweden was subject to the kings of Denmark. Under that system the most eminent of the nobles were appointed to administer the different provinces, and they exercised so much power in their separate principalities that they had reduced the office of guardian, or regent, or administrator, as he was variously called, to a position of comparative powerlessness. Charles, the lawful heir of the throne, inheriting the principles and guided by the policy of Gustavus, would by no means be contented with such a position. But inasmuch as the council approved this system—a system in which their own power and consequence would be enhanced—Charles was obliged to submit to it for the present, under emphatic protests, and with distinct assertion of his supreme power, under Sigismund, whom he represented, both as the heir to the throne and the regent of the kingdom. This was in fact, and it was so regarded, a notice to these lieutenants of the provinces that he should not allow himself to be a figurehead of the kingdom; but that he should assume and exercise supreme authority. The cunning device of Sigismund to limit the power of Charles by this arrangement, and the unwise acquiescence in it by the council, was the cause of the innumerable embarrassments in the administration of the kingdom to which Charles was

subjected during all the years previous to his own
elevation to the throne.

Meeting of the Estates. After an almost uninterrupted war with Russia for twenty-six years peace was at length
concluded, 1595, with that kingdom. But the turbu-
lent Clas Fleming of Finland refused to acquiesce in
some of the conditions of the treaty which referred to
that province, and still prosecuted the war. This led
to a convocation of the Estates. The duke had long
desired that they should be convened, under the conviction that he would be able to induce the three orders of
the knights and clergy and peasants to limit the powers
of the lieutenants of the provinces; but he had failed to
secure the assent of the Council. But now a crisis occurred—the virtual revolt of a province, whose continued war with Russia threatened to nullify the treaty
of peace—which made it an obvious necessity that a
diet should assemble.

But still the Council refused to join him in the summons, unless they were directed to do so by the king.
The Council and the Estates were positively forbidden
to assemble by the king. Charles in this crisis exhibited the boldness and the dominating power of his
character over those with whom he had to deal. He
presented the summons to them and told them peremptorily that they must sign it. "You must sign
the letters, and betake yourself thither too, or I shall
show you another way." He reminded them of Englebert the Dalesman, a peasant's son, but who as administrator constrained the council of the realm. "I am a
king's son," he said, "and prince hereditary of this
monarchy. After my will ye shall do, and if ye follow
not after with a good heart, I will have you brought
hither in bonds." They were compelled to subscribe;

but they still hoped that by the aid of the high nobility they could prevent any great change in their
own privileges, or in those of the lieutenants of the
provinces.

When the Estates assembled at Soderkœping the
duke took the same high tone with them as he had taken
with the Council.   It was only under a sense of duty to
the country and to himself, as the lawful heir of the
crown, that he had accepted the office of administrator
of the kingdom.   But as long as he held the office, he
insisted upon possessing the powers necessary to its
discharge.   If the conditions contained in the king's
oath at his coronation were not to be fulfilled, and if
Clas Fleming and other rebellious lords were not to
be punished, he would no longer occupy the position
of administrator.   And the Estates were now to decide
whether these two things were to be done.   The statute of Soderkœping, drawn up under the direction of
Charles, contained the following articles, which con-
stitute a declaration of absolute disobedience and defiance of the king; and were unanimously subscribed by
the Diet.   No doubt some of the subscriptions were
not *ex animo*.   The purport of the statute was as follows: That no other doctrine than that of the Augsburg Confession should be allowed in Sweden; that
even the natives of a different religion should be incapable of holding any office in the kingdom; that the
Popish priests should leave the country in six weeks;
that the Romish worship should be entirely abolished
not only at Stockholm, but at Protingsholm and Wadstena; that the nuns of the last place should be expelled; that for the future if any Swedes embraced any
other religion than the Protestant or educated their
children in any other profession, whether in Sweden or

elsewhere, they should be incapable of hereditary succession, their estates should be possessed by their nearest relations, and themselves banished from Sweden for ever. Those who had professed the Roman religion before the coronation of King Sigismund were allowed to remain in Sweden, though not to make any public profession of that religion, or to join in its worship, or in the celebration of any of its services.

To these decisive articles concerning religion, others relating to the duke's civil power, which were scarcely less stringent, were added. The duke should be Governor of Sweden, and in conjunction with the council administer all its affairs in the absence of the king; no suit or process which belonged to Sweden should be entered in Poland before King Sigismund; the right which every one had of appealing to the king could be exercised only when his majesty was present in Sweden; his majesty's orders sent from Poland to Sweden could not be published nor put in execution, till they were read and approved by Charles and his council. In the case of appointments which were invested in the king, the nomination should lie with the duke and the council.

It is obvious that these sweeping provisions absolutely excluded King Sigismund from the exercise of all power in Sweden except when he was personally in the kingdom. If we imagine such powers vested in the viceroy and council of Ireland, we shall see to what a nullity they would reduce the queen. They are to be vindicated only on the ground—and on that ground they are to be vindicated and applauded—of national self-preservation.

In order to give the utmost impressiveness to the assent of the Estates to these Articles, Chlares deter-

mined to hold what was technically called "a Bench
of Majesty." This "Bench of Majesty" was an elevated platform in the open air, immediately before
which the Estates were gathered, and around which
vast multitudes of the people thronged.   After an address to the Estates Charles addressed himself immediately to the people, closing thus: "After what we,
honorable and good men, both by means of the answers which ye gave us, on the points which were
propounded to you, have come to a clear resolution,
here therefore cometh my question, Whether ye mind
to defend what here hath been done and decreed, and
will stand to the same all for one and one for all, seeing it is grounded upon the oath and assurance of the
king, and nought hath been done save what is profitable to his royal majesty and to our fatherland." Yet
again he repeated the demand.   With that the common people answered, Yea, yea; yea gracious lord, and
took the oath with uplifted hands, to hold by his
princely grace all for one and one for all—which form
of speech the prince was ever wont to use.   Thereupon
he turned to the councilors of state, the bishops and
nobles, who stood by him upon the royal bench, and
questioned them in these words: "And ye, what say
ye to this?   Hear ye what these have sworn?   Will
ye sever yourselves from them?"   The council of state
answered in the name of the collective body of knights
and nobles, and promised to his princely grace obedience in all which should tend to the weal and profit
of king and fatherland.   But the prince raised his
hand and said: "So swear that ye will obey me in that
which I shall prescribe."   Then the greatest number
lifted their hands; but there were many who would
not.   Not from all, even in that position of command-

ing influence, could Charles obtain the pledge that they would obey him in all that he should prescribe. But the whole proceeding—the calling of the diet against the prohibition of the king and the refusal at first of the council—the thoroughness of its proceedings and the method of securing the adherence to both of the Estates and the people—exhibit the extraordinary resolution and ability of the duke. If at either of the two diets of Upsala, or at this, Charles had faltered, Protestantism would have been extinguished in Sweden, as, a century later, it was extinguished in Austria and Bohemia.

It would be an interesting topic for a monograph, by a competent historian—that of showing in how many instances the fate of nations, for centuries of weal or wo, has hung suspended on the fidelity and firmness, or the treachery and weakness, of a single mind. In such a treatise the history of Charles IX. would occupy a conspicuous and honorable position.

CHAPTER XII.

WE enter at this point into a new series of struggles and entanglements on the part of Charles, which it would seem that no one but a true inheritor of the stalwart body and the big brain and the indomitable resolution of the great Gustavus could for a series of years have endured.

Enforcement of the Ecclesiastical Provisions of the Diet. The statutes of Soderkœping were promulgated by Charles in Swedish and German and Latin. The worship of the Catholics at Stockholm, Drottningholm, and Wadstena, was interdicted and the priests were banished. The convent at the latter place, the most famous in the kingdom, was suppressed. A general church inquest for the suppression of Popery throughout the kingdom was established. The new archbishop, Abraham, drove on this measure throughout the kingdom with great severity; but no lives were taken on account of religion. The minister of the church of Stockholm, Eric Schepper, exhibited equal zeal. They were both violent, injudicious and unstable men; and when they found that they could not direct and overrule Charles they soon grew cool in carrying out the objects which they first advocated and pressed with undue heat. Schepper assumed to criticise and harshly censure some measures of the government which had no reference to religious interests. The archbishop protected Schepper; but his intervention did not prevent Charles's deposition of him from his office. To the archbishop he wrote, "We will maintain the right which our father of happy memory acquired, that it shall appertain to the magistrate to suspend a clergyman upon well-grounded cause from the exercise of his office; else might we as gladly sit under the Pope as under the Archbishop and Chapter of Upsala." The duke charged upon the archbishop that he demeaned himself more like an executioner than a paternal prelate.

Embassy from King Sigismund to Sweden. It was a matter of course that the proceedings of the Diet of Soderkœping should be very offensive to King Sigismund. He sent an embassy of six of his highest nobles to remonstrate against their execution. To their demand that these enactments should be rescinded Duke Charles gave a very decided refusal. These embassadors, however, had an opportunity to tamper with the members of his council, whose assent to the summons and the decrees of the Diet of Soderkœping we have seen were extorted by the firm measures of the duke. All of the members of the council but one joined with the embassy in demanding a repeal of some of the measures of the late diet, which they had sanctioned only under intimidation. Charles had now reached a point where he seemed absolutely helpless. Civil war raged in Finland. The commander of the troops in that country refused to lead them by command of the duke, while he himself was thus in open disobedience to the king. No other path seemed open to him but to resign. He

would not continue in office on condition of reversing,
or sanctioning the reversal of, the statutes of the Diet
of Soderkœping. Without this reversal, in obedience
to the king, he could not now secure the co-operation
of his council, or enforce the obedience of the leaders of
the troops. He resolved to resign. But the form in
which his resignation was offered leads us to infer that
he foresaw that an armed conflict in defense of Protestantism, which was now identified with the cause of
the old liberties of Sweden, was inevitable, and could
no longer be delayed.

The Duke Resigns the Government. When the duke announced that he would
lay down the government, he coupled with
the announcement the declaration that as
he had received it from the Estates, into their hands
alone should it be deposited. He accordingly convened a new diet to be held in February of the following year in Arboga. Meantime, on the 13th of January, 1597, came Sigismund's letter to the Estates of the
realm to the effect that he had learned from his envoys,
on their return, that the duke would not conform to his
directions: and that therefore the king transferred the
government of the country to the council. On the
25th day of the same month Charles wrote to the king
that the envoys had not mentioned to him that he had
already deprived him of the government. He then entered into a full vindication of all his proceedings as
those which were demanded by loyalty to the will of
his royal father Gustavus, and the principles upon
which he had established the government. He concluded with the statement that he had convened the
diet at Arboga; and with a declaration, which was in
effect an announcement, that whether that coming
diet should accept or decline to receive his resigna-

tion, he would still resist the efforts of the king to
overthrow the decrees of Soderkœping and to administer the government in the interests of Romanism.
The king could not misapprehend the meaning of such
a sentence as this: "We would not deal underhand, but
would have your majesty plainly informed and warned
that if the government of this realm be not otherwise
disposed and arranged (*i. e.*, otherwise than as you
propose) we will not be subject to such a government,
but will use those means and expedients which may
help for the alleviation of our own lot and that of the
country."

Diet of Ar- The conduct of Charles at first at Arboga
boga.   seems to sanction the conjecture which I
have made that he hoped that the diet would not accept his resignation. Finding that no one raised a
voice to dissuade him at the opening of the diet, from
resigning the regency, he retired to his near palace of
Gripsholm, as if for the purpose of taking no part in
its proceedings. But on reflecting upon the anarchy
that might ensue if he continued in that resolution,
he stifled his indignation and returned. The diet assembled at the designated time, notwithstanding the
prohibition of the king and the protest of the council.
One only of the lords of the council, Count Axel
Oxenstiern, could be induced to attend; and but a
small sprinkling of the nobility were present. Even
the hitherto too zealous archbishop was accused of
having secretly given in his allegiance to the king.
To the appeals of Charles the representative peasants answered with enthusiasm, and brandished their
clubs and axes in the face of the lords, declaring that
they would defend Charles, against all enemies, so
long as the blood was warm in their veins. The

statute that was passed was sent through all the country for signature. It contained a re-assertion of the statute of Soderkœping. Whoever opposed its provisions was to be put down by arms, as a public enemy; and the duke, who now, at the request of the diet, resumed the government, proceeded to the enforcement of its decrees. Most of the counselors fled from the kingdom. Charles, with great promptitude, took possession of Elfsborg, Stegborg and Calmar, and passed over into Finland where his old foe Clas Fleming had lately died. There he made several noblemen prisoners; and a new envoy of the king to Stockholm saw some of them conducted to the scaffold. The die was now cast; the issue was made; civil war already was begun. It was a distinct issue between a king who was attempting, against his coronation oath and the fundamental laws of the kingdom, to introduce a religion which they had repudiated and which they abhorred; and a prince, an hereditary heir to the throne whose foundation principle he was bound to conserve, and at the head of a people, for whose rights and liberties he was under the most solemn obligation to contend. There never was a clearer call of duty to self, to God, and to country, than that which was now made upon the duke.

Sigismund's return to Sweden. Upon hearing of these events the king raised an army of six thousand men and came to Sweden and took possession of Calmar. Even Stockholm declared for him. But Charles, at the head of the indomitable Dalesmen, who triumphantly bore the great Gustavus to the throne, prepared to meet the king in open fight. The presence of a foreign army in Sweden exasperated a large number of persons, who might otherwise have been neutral or friendly to the king. At a first encounter the forces of the king gained some advantage. But in a second great battle, at Stangbridge in Linkoping, the king's forces were utterly defeated, with a loss of two thousand men killed and comparatively few wounded; and with but little loss on the part of the army of the duke. The king and the duke held a personal conference immediately after the battle. This was followed by the convention of Linkoping, by which the faithless Sigismund was allowed by Charles, even in that hour of victory, to be acknowledged king on the condition, again renewed, that he would govern the kingdom according to his coronation oath, and send back his foreign troops, and within four months convoke a diet. From the general amnesty that was proclaimed Charles insisted that the names of five of the counselors, who had fled to the king in Poland, should be excepted. These lords were delivered up to the duke.

The ever-faithless king at once violated the provisions of the treaty of Linkoping by leaving a garrison of Polish troops at Calmar. By one of the articles of that treaty it was provided that the States should have the right to resist any violation of its provisions. Accordingly, when it was known that Sigismund had left these Polish troops at Calmar, the Estates assembled at Jenkœping in the early part of 1599 and renounced their allegiance to Sigismund conditionally. At a new diet in July this condition was withdrawn, and it was added that if within six months Sigismund should not send his son Vladislaus to Sweden to be educated for the crown in the evangelic faith, his family should forfeit for ever its hereditary right to the Swedish throne. The duke was declared reigning prince hereditary of the realm.

This was the end of Sigismund's power even in name in his hereditary kingdom.

Singular Position of Charles. According to the usual course of history it was to be expected that Charles would mount the throne. The Estates had declared that Sigismund and his heirs had for ever forfeited their hereditary right. Charles was the next acknowledged and undisputed heir. He had for a long time, during the absence of the king, administered the government; and now that the king's authority was disowned, his government of the kingdom with the full royal power would be continuous — uninterrupted and unshared. That he did not at once enter upon the office that was open to him, and did not subsequently, for a long time, accept it when it was pressed upon him, was not due to embarrassments and obstacles without, but rather to scruples of conscience which we cannot but regard as real. For his difficulties were increased by the singular and anomalous position which he occupied; and the peaceful settlement of the kingdom delayed by his persistent hesitation. While there was in the character of Charles a severity which subsequently, in the struggle with manifold treacheries, sometimes hardened into cruelty, there was at the same time a high conscientiousness, and a power of stern self-repression, and a vigorous will to follow out his convictions of duty, which recall the best specimens of heroic Puritanism. His religion was free from fanaticism, and was guided far more by moral than emotional forces. And along with this stern conscientiousness he had a lofty view of the prerogatives and rights of the house of Vasa, and would contend for their conservation, even when that contention would harm rather than help his personal interests. It is impossible to read the record of the career of Charles from this period with an understanding of its guiding principles and motives, except upon the view which I have here presented a view which Geijer has thus admirably explained and expanded.

"The common responsibility which Gustavus had imposed upon his sons was in truth Charles's political religion. Throughout his life he fought for the Swedish crown, seemingly against his own interest and that of his children; and he was himself, amid these contrarieties, torn by internal strife. With one hand battling against Sigismund, and all the dangers which with him threatened the country, with the other he struggled inexorably with the factions which had dared to beleaguer the throne of Gustavus Vasa. As the son of Gustavus, and from his whole position, he could not misappreciate the value of power bestowed by the voice of the people. But *on the same voice* his whole family rested their hereditary right. Against Sigismund, an outcast by religion from the heritage of the father of his line, Charles enforced the resolution of the Estates. But there remained a child whose weak arm, outstretched between him and the throne, seems to have excited in him deeper disquietude. Duke John, Sigismund's half-brother, was, by the hereditary settlement, his claim being unforfeited, next heir to the throne. Not only was the life of this child held sacred by a hand otherwise so blood-stained, but Charles fulfilled towards him all the duties of a near kinsman. He is still uncertain whether the young prince's renunciation of his pretensions, made at the age of fifteen, is valid; and closes by acknowledging in his testament John's superior right 'provided that the Estates of the realm shall in no wise depart from their enacted statutes.'

According to this Sweden was without a king at the
death of Charles, and first received one in Gustavus
Adolphus by a new election of the Estates."

By the light of this explanation of the singular
attitude of Charles's mind, we can comprehend some
of his proceedings after the deposition of Sigismund
which would be otherwise unintelligible. On the one
hand we cannot fail to respect the personal self-abne-
gation with which, in obedience to what he almost
alone regarded as a claim of right, he consented that
the crown should pass from his own gifted son to one
who had ceased to be a Swede, and had been educated
in the faith the attempt to introduce which into Sweden had convulsed the country for fifty years. On the
other hand we wonder at the seeming want of consis-
tency by which he adhered so fanatically to the principal of hereditary succession as to sacrifice his son's
pretensions to those of his nephew, which, by the
supreme authority of the State, had been forfeited;
while he left the kingdom in such a state as to make
it inevitable that his son should succeed, not by that
right of hereditary succession to which he rendered
such unusual homage, but by a new election of the
people. These are singular weaknesses in a strong
character which, although on the side of self-abnega-
tion, we find it difficult to respect, because they laid
his kingdom open to dangers, which all his life was
passed in the struggle to forefend and overcome.

Civil War. Sigismund's exasperation at the failure of
his effort to coerce Sweden was extreme.
He had enough partisans in the country, and especially in Finland, to excite a civil war. A slanderous
pamphlet was prepared against Charles, by the command of Sigismund, and distributed through all the

courts of Europe. The mutual animosities of the two
parties became greatly inflamed. The Dalecarlians and
the adjacent provinces were leagued to resist and crush
the partisans of the king. The lords of the council
who had been surrendered to Charles were tried and
executed. Many others were executed, and still more
banished. And while the war in Livonia and Finland
was in progress, in the conduct of which Charles ener-
getically intervened, the crown was twice offered to
him and rejected. The States indeed became impatient and angry with Charles because of this persistent
refusal of the crown. At length, in 1604, when the
civil war was ended, Charles accepted the crown after
it had been offered, at his request, to Duke John, and
had been declined on account of the conditions attached to its acceptance.

Relation of Charles to the Clergy and the Church. We have already intimated that Charles had
given some indications of his preference of
the Reformed to the Lutheran Church. His
relation to the clergy became unfriendly and
continued to be so to the end of his reign. It must be
confessed that there was not much in the character
of the Lutheran clergy at that time to secure the respect of one of such rigid principles, and such straight-
forward policy as Charles. Moreover, the Reformed
system itself, in its general principles, was no doubt
more congenial to his nature. "The perfecter of the
Reformation in Sweden," says Geijer, "was not reckoned an orthodox Lutheran." At the Diet of Linkœ-
ping, in 1600, a service-book prepared by him had been
rejected by the clergy. But Charles, notwithstanding,
introduced the new order of worship which he had
proposed into his own household. It was charged
that this service was Calvinistic; and the Archbishop,

Olaf Martinson wrote against it as such. It is curious to find among its alleged Calvinistic points, the
statement that heretics ought to be allowed Christian
burial. In the year 1601 Charles published a collec-
tior. of Swedish psalms. He also composed and published a collection of Swedish and German hymns.
In 1604 he issued a Swedish catechism, in which he
followed the Reformed catechism of Heidelberg. This
publication, together with his effort to secure an
amended translation of the Bible, caused no little
commotion among the Swedish clergy. Controversies
arose, in which Charles showed himself no mean polemic. He contended against the decree of a Diet
of Upsala, which had modified the article of the
Augsburg Confession, that the Scriptures were the
sole rule of faith. He also contended that sacraments
were only confirmatory signs of grace, and did not in
themselves impart forgiveness of sins. Hence he denied that the reception of the Sacrament of the Lord's
Supper at the hour of death was necessary for salvation, although it might be a comfort and support; and
he dwelt upon the anguish which was inflicted upon
the dying, who could not obtain the sacrament, by
this cruel dogma. He contended that only a condi-
tional and not a positive absolution should be pronounced upon confession; and that the words should
be inserted into the formula of absolution "in the
name of God who alone forgiveth sins." He also
advocated the use of reason and philosophy in the
construction of a Christian theology. It is creditable
to Charles, and in this we see an utter contrast to
the policy of his brother John, that he made no attempt to force his new services and doctrines upon
the diets and the people; and that the archbishop was

permitted to answer the royal theologian as an equal, without suffering any penalty or deprivation. The Lutheran system remained unmodified, and so continues in Sweden; and it must be confessed that it has exhibited itself there as narrow and intolerant as in any part of Europe. It is less than twenty years since the profession of the Catholic faith and the exercise of the Catholic worship has been allowed in Sweden.

Charles spent a large part of his life in the abortive attempt to unite the Lutheran and Reformed Churches. He did not adopt all the views of Calvin, and especially his most distinctive doctrine, the decrees of election and reprobation. Many conferences and disputations were held upon the subject. But all his efforts failed of making any impression upon the Lutheran clergy.

Concluding Years of Charles' Reign. The reign of Charles extended to the year 1611. During that period no new arrangements were made in ecclesiastical affairs. He devoted himself with earnest efforts to restore order and prosperity to the country; and his judicious and energetic measures for that object would have met with greater success, but for the wars in which he was involved with Denmark and with Russia. It is, notwithstanding, one of the enigmas of history, that, after so many years of strife and of national exhaustion which followed the death of Gustavus, a country so poor and sparsely settled should so soon afterwards develop the large resources and put forth the strength in the great Protestant struggle in Germany which has made the name of Gustavus Adolphus immortal.

THE END.